DRUG HATE AND THE CORRUPTION OF AMERICAN JUSTICE

DRUG HATE AND THE CORRUPTION OF AMERICAN JUSTICE

David Sadofsky Baggins

PRAEGER

Westport, Connecticut
London

Library of Congress Cataloging-in-Publication Data

Baggins, David Sadofsky, 1958–
Drug hate and the corruption of American justice / David Sadofsky Baggins.
p. cm.
Includes bibliographical references and index.
ISBN 0–275–95956–2 (alk. paper)
1. Narcotics, Control of—United States. 2. Drug abuse—Moral and ethical aspects. 3. Drug abuse—Government policy—United States. 4. Criminal justice, Administration of—United States. I. Title.
HV5825.B324 1998
363.45'0973—dc21 97–32946

British Library Cataloguing in Publication Data is available.

Library of Congress Catalog Card Number: 97–32946
ISBN: 0–275–95956–2

First published in 1998

Praeger Publishers, 88 Post Road West, Westport, CT 06881
An imprint of Greenwood Publishing Group, Inc.

Printed in the United States of America

The paper used in this book complies with the Permanent Paper Standard issued by the National Information Standards Organization (Z39.48–1984).

10 9 8 7 6 5 4 3 2

Copyright Acknowledgments

The author and publisher gratefully acknowledge permission for use of the following materials:

From *Smoke and Mirrors* by Dan Baum. Copyright © 1996 by Dan Baum; Afterword Copyright © 1997 by Dan Baum. By permission of Little, Brown and Company.

Excerpts from *Smoke and Mirrors* by Dan Baum. Copyright © 1996 by Dan Baum. Reprinted by permission of ICM.

To Aja Bea Baggins, age three, and Zachary Madison Baggins, working on one, with the hope that respect and tolerance best describe public policy for the long remainder of their lives.

Contents

Preface

Hate is a powerful organizing force in politics. Hate provides a distinction between "us" and "them" that allows a nation to define its nature and its cause. Inquisitions, crusades and prohibitions allow for powerful leadership to emerge and steer the nation toward a promised purity on a straight and narrow path that usually advances the particular interests of the ruling coalition.

Traditional white religious America came to feel under assault during the decades of civil rights marches, peace protests, and sex, drugs and rock and roll. Racial groups who once accepted their lesser status rebelled and assailed a segregated normalcy that was comfortable to many. Younger blacks suffered the full brunt of this deep lingering racism as incarceration rates soared under the authority of drug policy in following decades. The military, once the proud defenders against the communist menace, was ridiculed by a loud and often purposefully obnoxious dope-smoking peace movement. Many persons who defined themselves as patriots felt this behavior deserved harsh response. As the counter-culture receded, a new era of criminal "justice" accordingly set in. The federal government moved from patriotic defense of the orthodox American way of life in the 1950s to support of the underclass and avant-garde as the Great Society administered welfare and fed National Endowment grants to the arts community and intellectuals, many of whom were critical of and deviant from traditional values. The War on Drugs restored the former unliberal mission of government.

First in the hands of Richard Nixon, then Ronald Reagan, then many others, drugs became the metaphor for things wrong with altered American culture. Purposefully stoked intolerance toward drugs became both a symbolic and real means to fight against social change, enforce traditional culture and reinforce crumbling dominance relationships. Orthodox American culture used drug hate to legitimate a war on the unacceptable diversity and deviance in society. Politicians, the media, police agencies and government bureaucracies all joined in as this War on Drugs proved to have broad uses. The greatest use of all was to move the fundamental mission of government from redistribution and cultural enhancement under the banner of the Great Society to a conservative notion of the government as primarily a police force deployed in a state of righteous perpetual struggle with human sin.

The War on Drugs is the great public policy axis of the past two decades. It has controlled state budgets and agencies. It has proven to be the fundamental theme for contemporary reinterpretation of the Constitution. It has dominated political campaigns and the nation's information diet. It has also dominated intergenerational and interracial relations. It has molded the fundamental relationship of the people to the government and has deeply affected the life experience of millions of Americans.

Drug hate has become a meaningful form of patriotism for many. It provides a personal and religious expression of a wish for return to the days before the fundamental social changes of the second half of this century. As the century concludes it is well worth assessing the effects, causes, uses and rising forces of opposition to this American crusade. Drug hate is so deeply cherished a modern value that this search is an exploration of much of the social, political and institutional structure of the nation.

Chapter One begins that search in the deployment frontlines of the drug war. Criminal justice is the enforcement force of the nation's domestic crusade. Police, prisons, enforcement agencies, prosecutors and courts have all changed as institutions under the heavy weight of the War on Drugs mandate. Chapter One will show how these institutions as well as public policy and society are molded by this modern prosecutorial crusade.

Chapter Two turns to the betrayal of the nation's Constitutional heritage necessary to conduct this domestic culture war. The most basic ideas of due process, trial by jury, limits on police authority and promise of equal protection have receded to allow the drug war to be waged.

The judiciary, designed to be the people's active protectors of promised liberty, has been deputized as an extension of the prosecution effort in the name of the drug menace. The modern court was selected for their willingness to exempt criminal justice from the Bill of Rights. Their success, as detailed in Chapter Three, has been sweeping.

Chapter Four begins the search for the meaning of this self-declared domestic war. Drugs have held great symbolic meaning in this century. In the first half of the century drugs symbolized the contamination of this nation by foreign contact. Opium was criminalized out of fear of Asians. Marijuana was criminalized in an effort to neutralize the Mexican and black communities. Alcohol during Prohibition was associated with the undesirable ethnic European immigrants. Drug policy took a new twist as privileged white youths began to seek psychedelic exploration in the 1950s as means of breaking out of the taboos and narrowness of orthodox American culture. This became a massive counter-culture in the following decade which grappled for control of American civilization. Established dominant society fought back hard in the form of a genuine War on Drugs that persecuted deviance with as much vigor as ever in the nation's history. Drug hate became a greater phenomenon in the 1980s than drug culture was earlier. The War on Drugs became an expression of the nation's essential patriotism and religious belief.

Chapter Five considers the use of drug hate to particular beneficiaries. These include the politicians who roused that hate and then rode it to elective office, the media who sold the war between commercials as a graphic, sometimes bloody, made-for-television event, and a variety of government agencies who prospered under the shift in government mission. The War on Drugs has further uses in advancing racism, class hierarchy and an affirmation of orthodox American culture.

Eras come and go. Chapter Six looks at the evidence of deterioration of the hate zeitgeist that defined the conservative age as the animosity between liberal 1960s values and 1980s reactive values loses relevance in the nineties. Several politicians have learned recently that the hate card is no longer trump. Two initiatives suggest that the public is no longer captured by the hate wave. A norm of greater journalistic truth-seeking has substantially replaced the drug war media hype. European nations have ignored the American demand for a world drug war and enacted instead rational Harms Reduction policies that have proven to hold comprehensive superiority in outcome. As Americans examine their nation 30 years after the Summer of Love perhaps they find a culture too deeply changed to truly return to orthodox normalcy no matter how many prisons are filled. Can America's most costly and self-destructive public policy of the century be nearing an end?

It is my experience from my last two books that everyone around the author pays a price and is due an acknowledgment bordering on apology. My department at California State University at Hayward has become used to at least weekly moaning about the book and must be thanked for accepting my regular "that's a writing day" excuse. My wife, Teddi, has born the heaviest burden. Fortunately we have a lifetime together in which to make up for this lapse in our "go slow" philosophy. My children, Aja and Zachary, never did accept the excuse "Daddy is working" but nevertheless survived that as a daily fact of life. All my friends have come to accept that over the decade and a half that I have worked on the three books I would unpredictably exit a conversation as some matter of the text entered my brain for immediate exclusive processing. As always, with appreciation to my parents, Frank and Charlotte Sadofsky, who are always ready to listen. And to Moshe who is always ready to argue. Welcome Susan.

1

Drug Hate, Criminal Justice and Public Policy

Two national sets of data were placed before the public regarding criminal justice in 1997. Violence was down[1] while teenage and young adult illegal drug use was up.[2] Reaction to the continuation of these two long-term trends depends on personal orientation regarding the mission of criminal justice. Is the purpose of police, courts and prisons to promote a safer society or to punish forbidden behavior? The status quo of criminal justice answers that basic question with emphasis on protection of traditional morals through massive punishment of drug users and other persons engaged in forbidden vice. Denunciation of drugs and to lesser degrees pornography, prostitution, adultery, homosexuality and other traditional sins have dominated national rhetoric. Such crimes against culture exceed each of the other two categories, crimes of property and crimes against persons, as the dominant cause of incarceration today. Drug incarceration alone accounts for over half of the tripling of prisons since 1980. One thesis of this book is that criminal justice cannot begin meaningful improvement without recognition of the tragic and complex failures brought on by misplaced orientation as a tool for public morality. America's internal culture war both dominates and corrupts criminal justice as well as larger public policy and society.

In the 1990s, federal, state and local police units were exposed through a long string of separate investigations as being deeply corrupted. These investigations show both widespread vigilante lawlessness and broad involvement in the prohibited vice trades. In the 1980s and 1990s the cost of running the criminal justice system rose dramatically, even while America confirmed itself as the most dangerous and violent of developed nations. With the public's blessing, the mission of the public sector has changed from public projects and civic enhancement of the quality of life to one of commitment to punitive abundance. Incarceration has become the normal experience for the nation's young minority male population. Most striking of all is the abandonment in criminal justice of the Constitutional values that gave reason to the founding of the nation.

The condition of American criminal justice is both an effect of the dysfunctional war the nation has declared upon itself in the form of drug prohibition and a launching point for exploration of the depth of the drug hate phenomena. In the modern era the police were deployed on a cultural crusade. They were freed from the Constitutional restraints to vigorously pursue this difficult mission. The special burdens of vigorous sin policing and the economics of vice control coupled with the lack of Constitutional restraint, lack of meaningful judicial supervision and broad public cheering of invasive and brutal techniques to corrupt the police institutions and surrounding legal systems across the nation. To pay for the ever-larger wave of humanity caught in the criminal justice system, public spending has shifted from health, education, welfare and civic projects to punishment. The criminal justice system as dominated by the War on Drugs creates ever-greater shares of the public who are the product of incarceration, at ever greater expense, with ever-increasing hostility between the police and the target communities. This condition was brought on by public anger steeped in culturally based morality which was manipulated for political gain and economic profit to become the full War on Drugs. Before further examining the causes of the popular decision to become the world's most punitive country, consider in more detail the depth of the three costs of the war as measured in relation to criminal justice and general public policy. These themes are corruption of the police, shift from benevolent to punitive government, and social damage from punitive excess. That the nation bears these costs is an opening statement of how deep the drug hate phenomena runs in the nation's consciousness.

CORRUPTION OF THE CRIMINAL JUSTICE SYSTEM

A base level of corruption and misconduct is a given in every large organization. Police cannot realistically be expected to form an exception, though as the enforcers of the law, loss of integrity and subsequent loss of legitimacy makes police propriety unusually important. In the spectacular errors in Waco, Texas, and Ruby Ridge, Idaho, the nation's elite police forces were exposed as overzealous to the point of practicing lawless vigilantism. This is an exposure of conduct long ignored by the general population but also long known and experienced in the communities targeted by the Drug Enforcement Administration (DEA) and related domestic police agencies. A question of importance in reviewing these misguided police behaviors is, how have the police departments developed a sociology of warfare against segments of the American people? How have police officers, sworn to protect and serve, come to view the population of the nation as a hostile enemy?

In the Federal Bureau of Investigation (FBI) assault that resulted in the deaths of 80 Branch Davidian members living in an armed compound outside Waco, Texas, the country witnessed the wisdom of police conducting the public's affairs according to the Constitutional rules, and some of the potential cost when police fail to do so. In that instance the anxiousness of the FBI and Bureau of Alcohol, Tobacco and Firearms (ATF) to receive a warrant for a final assault led the police agencies to falsify claims against the sect. The agencies submitted reports of drug manufacturing and child molestation to their superior, Attorney General Janet Reno. The charge of drug manufacturing was subsequently shown to be baseless, and the charge of molestation was open to interpretation. Texas permits marriage at the age of 14, and by the Branch Davidian theology the whole community was a family. Through this use of wrong information the agencies received permission for the final engagement. In this raid most of the targeted community was massacred.

Initially ATF alerted the media of their intended raid so they could get their pictures taken as they successfully assaulted this non-conforming community. The members of the sect were warned by television news that they were about to be raided, so the ATF lost surprise as they opened fire on the armed community. They were then outgunned by the religious sect which the ATF originally sought to raid on a charge of weapons stockpiling. Even after the disaster no charges of perjury or disciplinary proceedings were brought.[3] Every one of the surviving members charged with murder for defending themselves against the assault was acquitted under a finding that the police deaths were justifiable homicides. As with much of this book, the behavior of the civilians was not pristine, and there is some basis for interest in their sociological deviancy, but the behavior of the police is far more reprehensible, and their sociology both more bizarre and far more important.

Two years to the day later, the country was reminded graphically and brutally of the cost of permitting such police brutality and of the ramifications of subsequent loss of legitimacy and vilification of government. On April 11, 1995, the bombing of a government building in Oklahoma City again stunned the nation. Observers of right-wing militia movements were not surprised to discover that the bombing was motivated by a will for vengeance in retaliation for police conduct in Waco.[4] As with all the major riots of the century, lawlessness by the enforcers of the law, when not corrected formally, yields tragic reaction. Police violence breeds community violence.

This mentality of the police at war with people of the nation was also played out in the national spotlight in the events at Ruby Ridge, Idaho. Again the victims of the police assault were highly unsavory. In this instance Randy Weaver, an alleged illegal gun dealer, promoted the cause of white religious-based racism and was implicated in the killing of a federal agent.

Again the behavior of the subject does not explain or excuse the behavior of the police. Again the police acted in a manner that was belligerent and morally repugnant if not criminal. In the 1992 standoff the federal agents gunned down the wife and son of their target.

The Senate subcommittee reviewed the matter and pondered the question of how the federal police had so lost restraint. "The Swashbucklers are in control" said Senator Charles E. Grassley, Republican of Iowa, complaining of what he called the "militarization of the F.B.I."[5] The Senate committee further learned that the federal agents destroyed documents in an attempt to conceal their vigilante behavior. Senator Arlen Spector concluded that the ATF falsified the record to construct an unconstitutional rule of engagement. He charged that they had falsified a criminal record for Randy Weaver and then attempted to cover up their behavior. Again acting in the name of duty, the federal police agency broke the law and compounded the sense of illegitimacy of police authority. Again, particular wings of the diverse American society interpreted the government's behavior as warranting disregard for government legitimacy. And so the reactionary National Rifle Association (NRA) issued a fund-raising letter to its membership describing federal authorities as "jack booted thugs."

These two stories are both representative in many regards and unusual as well. The representative portion is that the police acted outside the Constitutional limits on police authority to engage members of the public in a violent manner that rallied many others and robbed all police of some of their legitimacy. This loss renders future police work more difficult and typically even more vigorously confrontational, thus creating a spiraling cycle of abuse between the police and public. The unusual aspect is that the victims were white Americans not engaged in drug use. The many remaining examples to follow highlight both these similarities and differences from the more typical scenarios of police corruption and abuse.

Los Angeles, the nation's second largest city, tells the tragedy of criminal justice as well as any location. In the heady days of the Daryl Gates administration the Los Angeles Police Department (LAPD) embraced the rhetoric and substance of the War on Drugs. Accordingly, the LAPD strapped steel battering rams to military assault vehicles and began demolishing homes held by drug dealers. Daryl Gates achieved a level of national acclaim for his ruthless field work in this presidentially declared domestic war. Police Chief Gates himself was named policeman of the year by President George Bush. Weekly the LAPD conducted sweeps of gang youths and continuously raised the numbers of persons arrested, charged, convicted, or more likely plea-bargained, and sent to ever-expanding and -deteriorating prisons. During the Gates administration three-quarters of all young black men were at some time arrested by the LAPD. Of course the opinion held of the police and their chief inside the target neighborhoods was very different from the acclaim he received from distant sources.

This period of the War on Drugs as a public policy led to several foreseeable consequences in Los Angeles and elsewhere. First, the growing sense by police that the public is the enemy, a characteristic evidenced to the white community in Waco and Ruby Ridge but widely understood in poor and minority communities long before those stories emerged. As the recreational and economic behavior of a significant portion of the community became criminalized, no other relationship of the public to the police was possible. Second is a substitution of the mission of police work from public safety to cultural control. The focus of police authority, as during Prohibition, became the elimination of illicit vice. As during Prohibition, this mission caused the murder and violence rate to multiply. Recognition of public safety rather than elimination of sin as the legitimate and achievable goal of police authority would have accordingly refocused police resources away from the unwinnable mission. Tragically the nation became so captured by the rhetoric of domestic war that it stopped considering consequences. Third is the norm of disregard of Constitutional promises and citizen rights by the police. The text and spirit of the Constitution are substantially devoted to defining a limited role for coercive government authority with prescribed rules of procedure for police work. In periods where the police are ordered to achieve cultural control rather than public safety the Constitutional mandate becomes a distraction and so is discarded.

Fourth is loss of respect for the police in the communities targeted for control. When more than half the male teenagers in many neighborhoods are incarcerated, the idea of police as a friendly helper could not survive. So hostility of the police toward the residents of target communities is reciprocated by hostility of the community toward the police. This becomes a vicious cycle with no clear beginning of who started the violence and no end possible without clear and pronounced policy alteration. In this cycle of antagonism, where police recognize that their many assaults and arrests produce no worthwhile result, a norm of corruption sets in. Knowing they could never really win a drug war, soldiers of the war succumbed to its profits and allure.

These themes of failure became evident in the related L.A. stories of Rodney King and O. J. Simpson. Rodney King brought the organizational behavior of the Daryl Gates's police department to national attention. In 1991 the LAPD inflicted a two-minute severe beating on a black male named Rodney King. As in Waco and Ruby Ridge, the victim of this police assault was himself in the wrong. Also, like those instances, the behavior of the police was so reprehensible as to render the behavior of the victim irrelevant. Just after the release of the videotaped beating, a poll of Los Angeles residents reported that two-thirds felt such police brutality was common.[6] A different index of the lawlessness of the LAPD is offered by the 1,000 complaints of misconduct handled by the lawyer referral service each year and the 2,000 complaints registered with the internal affairs division.

Effective evidence of public discontent with the War on Drugs–era police brutality is found in the public outrage and riots following the rendering of a verdict of not guilty for the officers. This verdict was reached by moving the trial away from the jury pool of victims of police brutality to the sociologically insulated suburban Simi Valley. While the behavior of the police could be justified and perhaps appreciated in the suburbs, to many city folk the beating was a public rendering of an all too personal story of a police department at war with its captive community and unresponsive to the rules of legitimate use of authority. The flames and violence that followed the verdict can reasonably be seen as a tragic result of the misdirection of the police toward cultural control in substitution to the mission of public safety. Too many minority youths had personally experienced police brutality to remain unaffected by this taped public beating and the suburban jury's dismissal of the offense. The ultimate verdict against the police officers under the same facts when the jury selection came from city residents is one of the great demonstrations of the importance and potential of the jury system. Operating under the same facts, the Simi Valley suburban jury applied local experiences and norms to achieve a result opposite from that found by an urban jury applying different life experiences and sociology. The third trial, awarding $3.8 million to Rodney King in a civil action, again showed the sentiments of this urban public.

The L.A. County Sheriff's Office helped maintain the perception and reality of police as the enemy when they brutally invaded a bridal party of Samoan Americans. A $15 million jury award again demonstrated public sentiment.[7] So widespread is the perception of police as violent that 3 out of 4 instances of police shootings in L.A. result in a finding of police at fault.[8] Meanwhile the federal investigation of drug trafficking by the LAPD, Operation Big Spender, has convicted over a dozen officers.[9]

The O. J. Simpson trial brought to national attention yet again the ongoing tragedy of law enforcement in L.A. The defense in the trial perceived that the means to victory was to place the police on trial. Given the long history of illegal and brutal behavior of the LAPD, this seemed a strong strategy to argue before a primarily minority jury. The defense spoke of racism, perjury, and unconstitutional behavior. Then, upon investigation of the lead detective, the nation was presented in Mark Fuhrman with a personification of the complex failure of the police force.

Mr. Fuhrman by his own taped admission described brutal beating frenzies. One such account described a 1978 incident in which 16 officers joined in the mayhem. Fuhrman further described routine planting of evidence and other fabrications. The former LAPD officer elaborated on tape the police "kill parties," the pleasure they took in a "good beating," and his view of Constitutional criminal justice summarized as "most real good policemen understand that they would just love to take certain people and just take them to the alley and just blow their brains out. All gang members for one. All dope dealers for two. Pimps three."[10] The essential argument of this book is that such police stories are the fruit of inflammatory War on Drug and War on Crime rhetoric and policies. The only means to a more constitutionally acceptable police rule and a legitimate and effective police authority is to rewrite criminal justice mandates such that police are told to provide public safety and much less asked to forbid illicit sex, drugs and other elements of unapproved recreational behavior. As long as the principal mission of police remains vice preclusion, failure and corruption will remain the result.

Perhaps the most interesting aspect of the public reaction to the Simpson trial is offered in the deep difference in interpretation by race. Ninety percent of whites report belief in the police account while 90 percent of blacks do not. And so in the civil trial that followed, the white jury found Simpson liable. As with moving the Rodney King case to predominately white Simi Valley for jury selection, life experience and identity have much to do with level of trust. The victim classes have little. One minority observer commented, "The Furman tapes just confirm what black people in particular and people of color in general perceive: Law enforcement is institutional white supremacy."[11] Even before this revelation of racism 83 percent of blacks agreed that they could not trust the criminal justice system. In the 1960s the Kerner Commission concluded that conflict with the police set off every major riot. Police brutality set off the Watts riot in the 1960s. After the beating of Rodney King and subsequent riots, Chief Daryl Gates was replaced with the reform-oriented new chief, Willie Williams. The police union has resisted all his efforts for reform and in 1997 achieved his dismissal. Further tragic cycles of abuse and public reaction are inevitable.

Los Angeles offers a microcosm of the general tragedy of criminal justice, which is the message of this book. In brief, the story to be told in this book includes the following: the Constitution promises a model of police restraint in both its nature of mission and process; periodically throughout American history demands arise to alter the police mission to use police power to achieve cultural control—Prohibition is an archetype of such periods; from the 1980s through early 1990s has been a period of unprecedented commitment to such ends; police under the condition of the mandate of social conservatism have become corrupted; one dimension of this corruption is a widespread abandonment of Constitutional procedural rules. This misuse of criminal justice continues both because it speaks to social needs of the public and institutional and personal needs of those in authority.

New York, the nation's largest city, also offers its recital of this modern drama. In Manhattan's thirtieth precinct in 1994 a ring of officers stole a kilo of cocaine, marketed it on the street to the highest bidder, and got caught. Their arrest began an investigation that expanded to uncover a precinct in which crime among officers proved the norm. By 1996, 98 prior convictions were overturned because of police tampering with the evidence, there were 20 state convictions of police officers, and 18 federal convictions. An additional 35 officers are under indictment. Officers were reported to yield sufficient revenue from involvement in the cocaine trade that they plain forgot to pick up their comparatively small regular paychecks for months. A safe was stolen from a drug dealer, transported to the precinct, opened, and the contents divided among the police drug cartel. City investigations concluded that rather than accepting graft to look the other way to vice, police had become the oversight of the drug trade. The city is expected to pay over $10 million in settlement to perjury victims, many of whom are admitted drug dealers who were set up on false charges to allow police control of their trade.

So widespread was public knowledge of police misconduct that several hundred angry citizens met at the Church of the Crucifixion to demand city awareness of the brutal lawlessness practiced by the police. Prosecutors in New York report that they now have to screen potential jurors to determine if they are willing to believe anything a police officer testifies. They have found increasing difficulty seating a jury in which at least some of the members do not express the view that police routinely lie and coverup, and so their testimony must be discounted.[12]

Similar corruption stories in the New York Police Department (NYPD) were found in Brooklyn and the Bronx and in the city-wide special narcotic bureau. In the Bronx, as in Los Angeles, orders to prosecute the War on Drugs transformed into license for abuse, leaving the police as a brutal occupying gang in many neighborhoods. The Mollen Commission examined the systemic corruption in the Bronx and learned that officers "tuned up" suspects with their night sticks to coerce confessions. Citizen complaints of police viciousness rose in 1994 to more than 700.[13] Sixteen police officers were indicted in 1995 on such charges. Between 1990 and 1995 police officers cost the city $87 million dollars in restitution and litigation.[14] In the Riker's Island prison 26 officers have been charged with smuggling narcotics. As with the city and nation, there is a sharp cost in the corruption of police systems when criminal justice is used to forbid pleasure rather than deter violence.

Brooklyn revealed a particularly poignant instance of the reality of police corruption and consequent loss of legitimacy among the public. Three officers were acquitted by a jury of corruption charges. The jury felt that the officers testifying against their accused colleagues were not sufficiently trustworthy to believe even in this instance. The presumption based on community experience that officers lie as a Mark Furman–like code of conduct acquitted these corrupt officers.

The neighboring city of Philadelphia also partakes of the national experience. One police scandal after another has rocked Philadelphia in recent years. Calling for a war on crime and drugs was police heavy Frank (Attila the Hun) Rizzo. As elsewhere, the call for unleashing the police has produced a police department that is out of control. Agents have been shown to routinely falsify evidence, causing scores of cases to be dismissed. In 1996 160 police officers were reassigned in an attempt to break the pattern of abusive and illegal police practices. Five hundred more were scheduled for reassignment in continued effort to rid the police of its lawless culture.

A poster story of police mayhem involves Betty Patterson, age 54 and a grandmother who cleans homes for a living. In 1990 police officers framed her and falsely convicted her on crack cocaine charges. She served three years. Mrs. Patterson is one of the dozens, perhaps even hundreds, of victims preyed on by a band of five officers in her predominantly black neighborhood, through beatings, robbings, and indiscriminately plantings of evidence. The Philadelphia district attorney concluded that this was "the ultimate betrayal of the public trust."[15]

Outside Philadelphia on Interstate 95 a norm of stopping black motorists has exacerbated police-community relations. Three-quarters of persons arrested on the road are black though blacks only constitute 7 percent of road users.[16] According to the Supreme Court, characteristic-based, forced-stop policies of people who fit the description of drug carrier is Constitutional, despite the equal protection and Fourth Amendment implications.

Notable headlines in the city of "brotherly love" must include the reliability of police testimony in the case of Abu-Jamal and the decision to bomb the headquarter of Move. Abu-Jamal's case has attracted far more attention in Europe than in the United States. In Europe this prosecution of a radical black activist and news reporter for murder of a police officer is seen as evidence of continued use of criminal justice authority to oppress the black population. In the other instance, a radical black commune was subject to a bomb attack by the police which destroyed the site and the surrounding block. Several parallels to Waco are evident, including the illegal conduct of the victims and the far more reprehensible overreaction of the police. Only a police department that fundamentally saw itself to be in a state of war with the population is capable of such action. That is a very different mental orientation than a will to protect and serve.

Chicago joins the list of cities whose police became corrupt under the impossible mission of the War on Drugs.[17] There as elsewhere police officers have routinely planted evidence, shaken down drug dealers for protection money and acted as another gang on the streets. Seven officers from the city's West Side were arrested in 1996 on drug charges, and one turned out to be a member of an old street gang called "Vice Lords" that dominated local drug traffic. Other officers were simply found to beat up heroin users to pocket their $10 for the day's fix. They explained that heroin junkies were less than human, so why not take the dollars.

Miami continues the American story of police misconduct leading to social tragedy. The Miami area was particularly targeted as a hot spot for aggressive police action in the War on Drugs. The city erupted four times in the last decade, each time the result of police misconduct. The latest incident occurred in 1989 when a police officer shot and killed two black men. The resulting riot lasted three days and caused one death and millions of dollars in damage. Later that year the police lost a separate brutality case and were forced to pay damages estimated at $30 million. St. Petersburg, Florida also ignited as the community reacted to a police slaying in 1996.

The nation's capital was a particular victim of the War on Drugs allocation of resources away from the mission of public safety to public morals. The failure of police work there is infamous and a part of the national story. Billions of federal dollars were pumped in to build prisons. Incarceration rates sky rocketed to include half the teenage male black population. Murder rates in the city rose dramatically as the War on Drugs grew hot. Seventy percent of those murders were drug related. The solved murder rate dropped as police made vice their priority, falling from 3 in 4 solved in the early 1980s to 1 in 3 by the end of the decade. By 1993 a dozen police were arrested for corruption. The brutality rate predictably grew. In a highly publicized instance an adult black woman was handcuffed to a mailbox and beaten. Hundreds of prosecutions were subsequently dismissed due to proven police error and perjury.

A famous story of the experience of the federally prosecuted War on Drugs in the nation's capital is the targeting of the black mayor, Marion Barry. By intimidating a former girlfriend the authorities were able to tape the mayor indulging in forbidden narcotic pleasures. Yet so unpopular are the police and their war with the community that the public quickly reelected Barry to a new term as mayor.

New Orleans has fallen victim to the national police malady. Since 1992 more than 30 officers have received felony charges. Four of these are for murder. At the heart of the city's police problem is a department that long has accepted that it cannot successfully deter drug use or other illegal recreational activity, and so with a logic repeated throughout the nation the individual police officers have decided if you can't beat them, the police may as well join in the profit. Here too, the money of the drug trade and the raw sociology and economics of attempted prohibition of vice repeats its tragic consequence.

Pittsburgh joins in the national experience. In 1995, 5 suburban police officers grabbed a black man driving in a white neighborhood in an expensive car and beat him to death. Rather than a drug dealer he turned out to be a legitimate business man who was cousin to a Steelers football player. Marijuana was found in the car; the victim's family claimed the police planted it there. Tests showed the victim was not under the influence of alcohol or drugs, and television footage revealed the officers laughing at the scene of the death.

Even San Francisco, a city long blessed by a public morality of tolerance, has fallen victim to the deep dynamic of modern criminal justice policy. Though the city formally has declared recreational drug use to be the lowest priority of police affairs, they are still captive to the prohibitionist state and federal codes. And so in September of 1995 the largest police criminal conspiracy in the city's history was uncovered, as officers were indicted as accomplices of the drug trade. The city policy of allowing marijuana to be sold to AIDS (acquired immune deficiency syndrome) and cancer patients came under state assault when state agents raided the Cannabis Buyers Club in August of 1996. State officials, anxious to promote their own political futures, were simply unwilling to allow a city to opt out of the domestic war.

Detroit, rural South Carolina and Boston are also distinguished in levels of police corruption. The consequence of drug prohibition was a factor in each of these, as well as racism and a public demand for police work defined as a war on undesirables rather than professionalism under constitutional law. The tragedy of clamor by the public and politicians, leading to activist police-centered assault, leading to breakdown in police professionalism, corruption and, inevitably followed by loss of legitimacy and violent confrontation is a pattern that has swept most localities of the nation.

The national level is similarly corrupted by poor policy selection. The Drug Enforcement Agency, Central Intelligence Agency (CIA), and Federal Bureau of Investigation have all become corrupted by the drug prohibition.[18] Each have prosecuted agents for involvement in the prohibited trades. In 1996 the elite FBI crime labs were exposed to falsify their reports based on an attitude that it was the labs' job to back up the suspicion of agents rather than find the truth. As with local corruption, it is a matter of conjecture as to how much broader the unprosecuted corruption is than the prosecuted. In 1996 the *San Jose Mercury News* broke the story "Dark Alliance" of large-scale CIA complicity in Los Angeles' drug trade. The CIA has denied the claim, and Congress has announced its intention to conduct further investigation. When DEA Supervising Agent Clifford Shibata was indicted on 13 counts of embezzlement in 1996 he structured a revealing defense. "The DEA has incredibly sloppy record keeping, has no real system of keeping track of money used for informants in drug buys. They're trying to blame somebody."

REDEFINITION OF GOVERNMENT FROM HELPER TO PUNISHER

At the end of 1995 1.5 million Americans were captives of the criminal justice system. This placed the United States as the most incarceration-intensive nation per capita on earth with the only rivalry offered by the reborn nation of Russia with its vast problems of upheaval. If another nation utilized the extent of persecution the United States employs as prosecution, there would be broad condemnation regarding their tragic failure of human rights. When the 3.5 million other Americans under the control of the criminal justice system through probation and parole are added, the total of 5 million places the United States statistically squarely as the leading repressive regime on earth. This characterization is furthered with the addition of the 50 million Americans the subject of criminal files.

Approximately 6 million Americans are enrolled full time in all 4-year colleges and universities. The staggering fact of modern America is that it has chosen to punish nearly the same number of persons it has provided the opportunity for a higher education, and at greater expense. From 1987 to 1995 spending on state prisons rose 30 percent, while higher education funding fell 18 percent. In 1995 state spending on prisons rose to $2.6 billion, while state spending on construction for higher education fell to $2.5 billion.[19] In the great guns versus butter tradeoff in our day, we implicitly choose domestic guns, mostly directed to the punishment of non-violent cultural offenders, over opportunity for personal growth and economic betterment. The great question of public policy in our age is why the nation has chosen to provide so little positive opportunity while investigating in so much hurt? What has made anger rather than a will to build and aid the guiding force of policy and politics? That is the topic of Chapters Four and Five.

The commitment to punishment as the focus of public expenditure is only growing. In 1995 the total number of inmates grew by 1,600 a week. That was a 9 percent increase from the high levels of the prior year. The Republican contract with America called for federal funds to induce states to build more prisons and required for these funds that 85 percent of sentence duration be served in incarceration. An array of mandatory sentencing laws can only exacerbate the trend. The Drug Policy Foundation calculated that the War on Drugs directly cost the tax payers $30 billion in 1996. Total economic cost for that year is estimated by the *National Review* at $75 billion.[20]

California has led most social trends of the century, from free love and drug culture in the 1960s, to the proposition 13 anti-government taxation revolt in the 1970s to prison construction in the 1980s, to the Three Strikes incarceration initiative in the early 1990s, to the anti–affirmative action initiative in the mid-1990s. All of these movements held powerful reverberations for the rest of the country. They all need to be understood to fully appreciate the culmination in the War on Drugs as a focal commitment of an age.

As the once-aggressive counter-culture of the state lost direction and energy, California elected a string of politicians who campaigned for the criminalization movement, politically marketed eventually as the War on Drugs. The theme of political reasoning stated that it was necessary to expand punitive government to reduce violence and restore good traditional culture. Ronald Reagan as Governor, later President, was a principal author and beneficiary of this strategy. Denunciation followed by incarceration became the relationship of the government to the counter-culture and to selected ethnic minorities. Positive government shrank as limits on taxation set in; punitive government grew as the replacement commitment.

From the gold rush to the formation of Hollywood, California has long dared to do things on a grand scale that have shaped the nation. With economic and population growth in this century, public works projects became the focus of the golden state. In the 1930s the public sector constructed the water systems that allowed cities to rise from scrub lands and made farms of the desert. After World War II public energies went into public higher education, building the nation's largest and for a time best public research and education system. This energy was devoted from the 1950s on to construct a freeway system mammoth in its proportions. By the mid-1990s the freeways stood clogged, the universities scaled back their ventures under unprecedented financial pressure, waterworks and public lands acquisition were a thing of the past and prisons emerged as the new massive commitment of public expenditure. The prison boom in this conservative era rivaled in scale any of the past grand ventures.

Only the nations of China, Russia and the United States as a whole can boast a bigger prison system. No public entity has a better financed punitive system. In 1996 government spending on incarceration surpassed spending on the once lauded University of California, California State University and community college systems combined.

In 1983 there were about 35,000 inmates in California state prisons. In 1995 there were about 150,000, two-thirds of whom were black or Latino. With the Three Strikes initiative this number is expected to pass the 200,000 mark by the year 2000. Annual cost of operating the system in 1995 approached $4 billion. Because of lack of assets to continue the drive for new prison construction, an elaborate and financially silly scheme of leasing prisons built for the state and bond issuance against an enterprise that has no economic return has become routine.

In 1978 the California penal code was rewritten in recognition of the truth that rehabilitation is not the product or purpose of this mass incarceration system. Punishment as retribution for breach of the law became recognized as the sufficient reason for prisons. Discretion was removed from judges in that same year in the form of mandatory sentencing. Since then over 1,000 laws were enacted mandating ever-increasing sentences. All this kept population pressure on the punitive system. The Three Strikes initiative multiplied the state demand for punishment. According to the Rand Corporation this initiative, sentencing persons convicted of a third offense after two serious crimes, will double total incarceration in a decade. The legislative analyst office expects that in order to maintain the 180 percent of capacity overcrowding currently practiced in California prisons, 15 new prisons will need to be constructed by the year 1999. If these prisons could be built on state appropriations, the cost is estimated at $4 billion. Since that money cannot be found in the budget, financing will increase the costs of these projects. Operation adds more cost. The Rand Corporation estimates that prisons will constitute 18 percent of the state budget by 2002. Since under Proposition 13 the state cannot raise revenues, the funds will necessarily require cuts in other services; therefore, transfer from education is the likely source for this revenue. The State Supreme Court in 1996 rebelled against the clause of Three Strikes that gives prosecutors discretion but strips courts of the right to refrain from imposing this mandatory minimum law. It is not clear how this judicial decree will affect the projections or if the legislature will find a way to overturn this ruling.

The massive shift of budget resources to incarceration and away from education has three important implications for the state and nation. First, limited education is a leading correlation to violent and property crimes, though not to drug use. Withdrawal of funds from education feeds the supply of new individuals statistically inclined to become criminals, expanding the punitive state. Further, limited education on the part of the electorate is the leading correlate to demand for more punishment as means to restore traditional values.[21] Hence greater ignorance increases the voting base, demanding more angry punitive orthodoxy enforcing government, thus building the War on Drugs. The will to use punishment to restore a sense of well-being among people who think themselves losers in American culture is the focus of Chapters Four and Five. Third, as resources are shifted away from service-oriented government to punitive government there is a shift in lobby capacity and citizen expectation. The union of prison guards has emerged as the second biggest source of campaign contributions in California. Their 1994 contribution to the punitive-enthusiastic Governor Wilson was the largest in state history. The governor placed in his budget that year an 8 percent pay increase for prison guards. This job requires only a high-school education and already pays in the mid $40 thousand in average salary. The correction officer's union provided the seed money for the passage of the Three Strikes initiative, guaranteeing increased demand for punishment services. Thus far participation in the forbidden marijuana trade, the state's leading crop by cash value, is the largest basis for Three Strikes sentencing.

All of this commitment to punishment has required significant shifting of resources. California spent 2 percent of its state budget on prisons in 1980, and 9 percent in 1994. In 1996 the Governor's budget proposal again called for a major new increase for corrections. California has added 18 new prisons since the mid 1980s to a total of 30. The average cost per inmate is over $20,000 per year. Average cost of imprisoning an inmate over 50 with health problems is $60,000. Due to mandatory longer sentences, the number of older and so costlier inmates is rising dramatically. Stripped of the ability to make personal judgments by mandatory sentencing laws, the state's prisons are forced to develop extensive geriatric facilities, housing persons highly unlikely to commit violent offenses if released to live out their remaining lives at home.

The non-partisan legislative analyst of California conducted a review of the Three Strikes law a year after implementation. His conclusion is that the Three Strikes initiative has clogged the courts, packed the jails and resulted in the early release of violent prisoners to make way for mandatorily incarcerated persons. The most common crime to receive a Three Strikes sentence is cultivation of marijuana, which as a category exceeds all violent crimes combined in persons incarcerated. This commitment to punishment of such vice crimes is only comprehensible once criminal justice is seen as more about a fight against bad culture than as a means to raise public safety.

California is at the lead of this social trend of redefinition of the public sector away from health, education and welfare toward punishment as the public commitment and growth activity. The nation as a whole is not very far behind. In the last 15 years the nation's prison population has tripled. One and a half million Americans are incarcerated, over 5 million Americans are under the control of the criminal justice system, there are 50 million subjects of criminal justice records in the nation's data banks. There were over a half million arrests for marijuana possession in 1995. Marijuana has emerged as the nation's leading crop, valued at $32 billion dollars a year. This will toward punishment has profound social consequence in the relationship of citizens to the state and toward each other.

THE SOCIAL HARM OF MASS INCARCERATION

Through the laws of mandatory sentencing, criminalization of recreational drug use and other sins, Three Strikes laws and high penalty laws, society has lost its ability to utilize punitive resources strategically. It is this inability to think about crime strategically and to punish rationally that drives the complete lack of correlation between spending on criminal justice and public safety. The inability to introduce rationality into the infliction of punishment has created a vast class of nonviolent criminals and inmates.

Throughout the nation, spending on criminal justice surged throughout the last two decades, yet violence rose with police spending throughout the 1980s then peaked in 1992–1993 and began to decline. The shift in drug patterns away from crack and back to marijuana and speed, along with the ageing of the baby-boom generation and drop in persons 16 to 24 years old go much further to explain the decrease in violence in the years 1993–1997 than any use of punitive authority. Among the ten largest cities, New York and Houston added more police and observed reductions in violent crime, but Chicago hired record numbers of police and violent crime grew, while San Diego reduced both police and crime. The Sentencing Project associate director concluded "Inmate populations have quadrupled in 20 years, but I don't know anyone now who feels safer than 20 years ago."[22] What can be said of this period is that record numbers of persons were incarcerated, and violent crime as well as recreational drug use were remarkably unaffected. Inmate population rose 213 percent between 1980 and 1994. During this time recreational drug use fell in the 1980s then rose in the 1990s while violent crime rose in the 1980s and fell in the 1990s.

Why is there so little observable benefit in spite of the mass incarceration? One answer lies in examining for whom and for what crimes society constructed prisons. There is demonstrable incarceration utility to locking up some offenders, particularly violent criminals and habitual burglars and robbers. Unfortunately whatever measurable utility results from such action is diluted to the point of irrelevance by the large numbers of persons incarcerated for cultural offences. Sixty percent of all federal prisoners are drug offenders, up from under 25 percent in 1983. Half the growth in state and federal incarceration from 1980 to today are drug criminals. Each year the nation makes over a million drug arrests, yet drug use continues to climb. There is near to no incarceration utility to locking up drug users as measured by change in drug use. According to the Michigan Institute for Social Research, over half of all high-school seniors have used illegal drugs in 1996, up by 6.7 percent from 1991. The idea that the nation could or should make prison space available for this share of its youth is absurd. High-school students and the nation clearly benefit more from a college experience than from prison. Occasional experimentation with drugs is correlated positively with academic performance as measured by college admission. Average federal prison sentences for all drug offenses has risen to 86 months, while the average is only 92 months for all violent offenses. Fifty federal judges have announced that they will not hear any more drug cases, both because the volume of such prosecutions choke their courts and in protest against the laws that prevent reasonable levels of punishment for trafficking and indulgence in drugs. The number of drug arrests in 1993 by both state and local police was 1.1 million. There have been 4 million marijuana arrests since 1980. Because these cases carry so much worthless expense and activity, it is understandable why the massive funds to criminal justice have yielded so little social gain and have produced so much real harm.

The one conceivable benefit to incarceration of recreational drug users is if prison succeeded in promoting sobriety. Yet for all society's will to incarcerate, rehabilitation has exited the prison experience. Texas under Governor Ann Richards established a model drug and alcohol treatment program, which was eliminated by her replacement, George Bush, son of one of the presidents sponsoring the War on Drugs.

The statistics on the immense failure of the War on Drugs is the important base for the overall failure of all criminal justice. Two basic points need to be understood in this regard. Illegal drug use has proven impervious to prosecution as a deterrent. As the devastating health consequences of tobacco use does not deter tobacco consumers, so too the far less certain punitive wrath of the state does not deter other drug users. After a decade of mass incarceration, occasional recreational drug use, particularly by the young, remains common. The only benefit of incarceration in the War on Drugs is if it makes cultural defenders feel good. This benefit, to the degree it exists, is achieved at immense cost. Second, the principle allocation of punishment resources to cultural deviance has created a vast class of post-incarceration humanity.

Real fault in criminal justice lies in the criminal code itself. The criminal code should be the product of public policy analyses fairly measuring the utility of incarceration among the array of behaviors sought to be discouraged. Instead it is the repository of culture preferences and angers. The standing criminal code has created a nation with millions of Americans holding criminal records. Each year there are another 12 million misdemeanor offenses. More than 5.1 million Americans are incarcerated or otherwise under control of the criminal justice system.

The failure of strategy in criminal justice was vividly played out in the nation's capital. With great fanfare the George Bush administration announced that national resources would be targeted at the local drug market. Prisons were built, and over one-half of the city's male teenagers were incarcerated. In synch with the national experience, the murder rate soared. The percentage of solved murders moved from 3 in 4 in 1980, to 1 in 2 in 1988, to 1 in 3 in 1989. Seventy percent of the killings were drug related. As with the nation as a whole, murder rates did not fall until the illegal drug markets sufficiently stabilized to replace violent turf raiding with more structured criminal organization.

In studying the linkage between illegal drug use and violence, Scott Decker, professor of Criminal Justice at the University of Missouri, proved that users of drugs are no more likely than other people to carry and use guns. So mass incarceration of them does not reduce violent crime and diverts resources. Drug sellers, alternatively, do contribute to the epidemic of guns and violence. And so the creation of criminal markets through the criminal codes is a root cause of violence.

To produce a strategically rational criminal code involves two essential issues in allocating expensive incarceration resources: the replacement effect and the incapacitation effect. This is to say, incarceration is effective to the degree that no new person replaces the activity of the incarcerated person and the incarcerated person would have performed more of the criminal act but for incapacitation. Prostitution is a clear example of an area in which the replacement effect holds the value of incarceration to zero. If a supplier of sexual services is incarcerated, the buyers seek and finds alternative suppliers. Hence despite centuries of intermittent prosecution, the market transcends deterrence by continuously engaging new practitioners.

Drug use has proven to be impervious to impact through incarceration. Incarceration destabilizes the market briefly, leading to violence as market segment is fought for, then as new producers and sellers succeed the market comes to new equilibrium. Society has only prevailed in expanding the web of criminality as it now holds the original dealers and users, incarcerated or released with a record and a period of parole, and the new entries drawn into the market. There is even surprisingly limited incapacitation effect, as prisoners find the means to continue their illegal recreational drug use in drug-permeated prisons.

Research by the Rand Corporation shows there to be a real and positive incarceration effect in the area of burglary. When burglars are incarcerated, fewer burglaries are subsequently observed. This reduction in burglaries is in part explained by the strong tendency of burglars to engage in repeat acts. Once persons develop the skills of burglary, including entry, identification of valuables, and conversion to cash, they practice the skills repeatedly. Normally each burglar commits 70 acts each year.[23] The incarceration of a burglar does not invite new burglars to market entry. Burglars do not have market niches that cause the value of burglary to rise with incarceration of the established practitioners.

These elements of strategy require the conclusion that society deploy its limited and expensive incarceration resources to those areas of crime that yield reductions in the incidence and burden of crime to the public. In essence, crimes with victims are usually subject to reduction while crimes against culture are not. The Drug Policy Research Center demonstrated just this point by showing that the spending of a million dollars on longer sentences for convicted drug dealers would reduce the nation's total consumption of cocaine, estimated between 276 and 321 tons each year, by less than 29 pounds a year. That is almost no return to the dollar, yet the system continuously generates expansion of such incarceration.

The statistics in New York State demonstrate the lack of rationality in use of punishment. In 1997 the governor asserted that the state needed 8,000 new prison beds to hold violent criminals. However, the state had experienced a drop in violence and so spaces were increasingly occupied by low-level drug dealers and users. Since 1983 the percentage of violent felony commitments fell from 63 percent to 29 percent of those entering prison. The percentage of those entering for drug offenses rose from 12 percent to 46 percent in 1996. If the state only prioritized prison space to violent criminals, it could further reduce violence and save great amounts of money.

That society has deployed its resources exactly opposite of strategic rationality suggests either mass stupidity or that reduction of violence and other real harm is not the purpose of criminal justice authority. This alternative hypothesis itself requires explanation. If the criminal code is not meant to primarily produce safety, then what is its product? One answer has already been given. Illegal drugs may be safer from a public health perspective than alcohol and tobacco, but they carry elements of counter-culture, ethnic diversity and deviance. The criminal code serves as a mechanism to try to affirm traditional culture within a population that is significantly broader in its behaviors and sociology. This role of cultural enforcement is similarly suggested in the punishment of sexual conduct, pornography and prostitution. Emphasis on criminal justice as means to cultural purification is a big portion of why the Constitutional promises regarding limitation of police power have so thoroughly retreated. Lack of social rationality in the deployment of criminal justice resources is further explained by consideration of who does benefit from public policy emphasis on crimes against culture.

The lack of strategic restraint in infliction of punishment has exacerbated both the nation's race problems and its disparity of wealth. Three-quarters of new admissions to prison are now black or Latino. By 2010 if current trends persist, the absolute majority of all 18–40 year old nonwhite males will be in prison. American prisons are now composed of over half blacks, and only 18 percent whites. Blacks are incarcerated at the rate of 1432 per 100,000 persons compared to whites at 203. Blacks are 12 percent of the nation and 54 percent of the prison population. Blacks constitute 13 percent of illegal drug users yet receive 55 percent of the convictions and serve 75 percent of the prison time. Criminal justice has replaced segregation which itself replaced slavery as the nation's real race policy.

Despite evidence that large numbers of whites indulge in drugs other than the traditional use of alcohol and tobacco, law enforcement targets blacks. The U.S. Sentencing Commission study shows 96 percent of federal crack defendants are nonwhite. Mostly they were lookouts and street dealers rather than kingpins, who are rarely prosecuted. When arrested, nonwhites in L.A. are sent to federal prosecution where they receive the 10-year minimum sentences, whites receive state prosecution and average less than a year of incarceration. Crack, predominantly a poor person's drug, is punished at 100-fold compared to real cocaine, a middle-class drug, despite the basic ingredient of crack being cocaine. Persons arrested with crack are subject to mandatory minimum terms with a presumption that the user is a dealer. Crack is the only drug with a minimum sentence. The national average time served for murder is 8 years, rape 5 years, robbery 3 years, but the average sentence for a crack conviction is 11 years. This disparity in treatment is a cause of the incarceration of over one-third the black males in their 20s in California.

Prisons are both America's contemporary response to poverty and a significant factor in the creation of that poverty. A third of prisoners were unemployed the year before incarceration. Only half were employed full time, 75 percent of those employed earned less than $15,000 and one-third earned less than $5,000. After incarceration there is a 25 percent reduction in ability to find work. Yet society finds increasing resources for incarceration but decreasing funds for job training and work programs.

Jeffrey Groger, an economist at the University of California at Santa Barbara, explains that first-time arrestees saw income drop by 7 percent after release. This lowering of earning potential necessitates return to crime. By doing worse economically when they are released, former inmates become multiple offenders. In his study of disadvantaged youth ages 17–22, a 10 percent drop in pay yields 6 percent increase in crime. By raising return to labor this progression into habitual criminal cycles could be reversed. Low education achievement is also a significant explanation of who receives incarceration. In a 1991 survey, 65 percent of prisoners failed to complete high school. Spending on schools in low-income areas is an effective means of retaining students and increasing income potential. But the will in society is for punishment, not effective social progress. The modern focus on punitive government is a cause of social decline.

Modern criminal justice is dominated by the commitment to the War on Drugs. This commitment has corrupted the law enforcement agencies, shifted public spending from programs that build society to mass incarceration, and has led to a civilization damaged by the sheer number of persons who have experienced incarceration without compensating benefit to society from their sentence. None of this is unknown. The powerful questions are, how has this all happened in a nation whose Constitution was written largely to limit police abuse and why are such self-destructive policies demanded by the nation.

NOTES

1. *Annual Survey of Violent Crime* (Washington, D.C., Federal Bureau of Investigation, 1997).
2. *22nd National Survey of Licit and Illicit Drug Use Among Teenagers*, University of Michigan Institute for Social Research, January, 1998.
3. Senate Judiciary Committee, *Waco Hearings*, 103rd Cong., July 19–30, 1995.
4. *Waco: The Rules of Engagement*, Directed by William Gazecki, 1997.
5. "Theatrical Threshold Adorns Hearings on Idaho Shootout," *New York Times*, Sept. 7, 1995.
6. "Video Taped Beating by Officers Puts Full Glare on Brutality Issue," *New York Times*, March 18, 1991.
7. "Party Goers Win 15.9 Million in Suit Over Melee," *Los Angeles Times*, Aug. 8, 1995.
8. "LAPD Officers Faulted in 3 of 4 Shootings," *Los Angeles Times*, Aug. 14, 1994.
9. "Drug Officers Corruption Case Ruled a Mistrial," *Los Angeles Times*, March 6, 1992.
10. "The Fuhrman Tapes and the L.A.P.D.," *New York Times*, Aug. 20, 1995.
11. "The Tapes Simpson Wants for the Jury," *New York Times*, Aug. 23, 1995.

12. "Jurors Question Honesty of Police," *New York Times*, Sept. 25, 1995.

13. "Bronx Abuse Complaints Stir Crackdown on Police," *New York Times*, May 2, 1995.

14. "The Cost of Police Brutality," *New York Times*, April 22, 1995.

15. "Philadelphia Shaken by Criminal Police Officers," *New York Times*, Aug. 24, 1995.

16. "The Second Casualty of War: Civil Liberties and the War on Drugs," Paul Finkelman, *Southern California Law Review*, Vol. 66, pp. 1389–1422.

17. "Worst Fears Are Realized With Officers' Arrests," *New York Times*, Dec. 30, 1996.

18. "Call for C.I.A. Cocaine Inquiry Is Renewed," *New York Times*, May 15, 1997.

19. Justice Policy Institute, 1997 Annual Report.

20. William F. Buckley, "The War on Drugs is Lost," *National Review*, Feb. 12, 1996, p. 35.

21. Tom Tyler, "The Psychology of Public Punitiveness: The Antecedents of Public Support for the Three Strikes Initiative," Unpublished Lecture, Dec., 1997.

22. Marc Mauer, The Sentencing Project, *1996 Annual Report*.

23. Rand Corporation Study, "The Utility of Burglar Incarceration," 1996.

2

Constitutional Limits on Police Authority and the War on Drugs

If the content of the Bill of Rights were analyzed word by word and classified by subject, limitation of police powers easily emerges as the dominant theme. Consider that of the 10 amendments that form the charter on liberty, the Fourth, Fifth, Sixth and Eighth Amendments specifically describe limitation on the process of criminal justice. The First, Second, and Ninth Amendments limit the range of subject matter that the government is permitted to forbid. Of the 26 separate rights specified in the first 8 amendments, 15 are specifically aimed at the criminal process, and many of the remaining 11 have criminal law implications. Given this textural centrality, definition of police power emerges as one of the central themes of the Constitutional legacy. Given the abusive history of deployment of police power by kings, governments and churches to forcibly control their captive societies and neutralize opposition and deviance, this emphasis on limitation of police power to create a more free and just society is both understandable and wise.

Examination of the model of criminal justice articulated in the Constitution is the theme of this chapter. Such review is conducted both to appreciate the importance of limitation on police power to the Constitutional promise and to offer some measure of how far from this promise modern America has strayed through its will to use prosecution to reform civilization. Key to the argument of this book is the belief that an essential means to ending the tragedies of American criminal justice is restoration of the Constitutional promises.

A reasonable place to begin discussion of the Constitutional ideal is with trial by jury, a facet of the Constitution drawn from the European experience, violated by the king and colonial government, demanded in the Declaration of Independence, written into state constitutions and repeatedly promised in the text of the Constitution. Like most Constitutional promises, it stands routinely violated by the modern dysfunctional will for mass incarceration.

The right to trial by jury is a centerpiece of Magna Carta. King John of England became oppressive, as rulers tend to, and the barons rebelled. In 1215 the king accepted their great charter as a limitation on his power. This charter codified the claim that some customs had an authority that exceeded the power of the king. Article 35 stated that "no freeman shall be arrested or imprisoned . . . except by the lawful judgement of his equals and according to the law of the land." In demanding the right to a jury trial the authors were invoking an ideal that was practiced in England from the time of the Norman conquests and which dated in Europe back to the rule of Charlemagne.

These limitations, which the king was forced to codify, were concessions of sweeping importance. If police power is held in monopoly, then the king or state can use it to coerce any manner of behavior. If the people are invested with the ultimate authority to declare guilt or innocence, they then possess a veto on oppressive use of the police power. Juries through a tradition subsequently known as jury nullification can simply refuse to convict in any matter they consider oppressive or immoral. Repeatedly through the Western legal traditions governments have sought to violate the promise of trial by jury so as to consolidate ruling authority through police power. Also repeatedly the people have used the jury power to resist oppressive laws and administrations.

A historic example of the latter is provided in the trial of

William Penn. The Conventicles Act forbade worship other than that performed according to the Anglican form. Thus the church that recognized the king as God's emissary on earth was given a monopoly by the state over religion. William Penn in 1670 stood charged with unlawful assembly and breach of the peace for addressing a group of Quaker worshipers who were locked out of their Friends Meeting House by soldiers. The warrant, drawn before he began to speak, charged him with "preaching seditiously and causing a great tumult of people on the royal street to be there gathered together riotous and riotously."[1]

Penn and his associate conceded the facts of the case but argued justice to the jury. Penn proclaimed his "indispensable duty" to worship God. The judge took the side of the state and official church by admonishing the jury that the common law forbade the speech of Penn and that they had no right to question the law. Penn renewed his argument that the jury should question the righteousness of the law as determined by the court. The judge labeled Penn as "pestilent" and had him removed from the proceeding. As he was dragged off, he pleaded to the jury to assume the role of final judges in equity and to use their consciences to rule on the matter.

The jury and the court then entered into a contest of wills. The jury, caught in conflict between the text of the law and their opposing conscience, did not wish to render a verdict. The court insisted that they rule. The judge held the jurors in confinement without food until they completed their task. Ultimately, despite court instructions to find Penn guilty, the jury voted their conscience and reached a verdict of not guilty. The court accepted the verdict and fined the jurors for their disobedience to the court and the written law. This fine was contested and eventually overturned, enhancing the power of the people through the jury format to claim the power of nullification and find law and prosecution morally unacceptable.[2]

The William Penn legacy is important because it is a case study of the essential dynamic of abuse made possible by the state holding police power and protection from such abuse offered by the jury system in criminal justice. The government found reason to believe that control of the nation was facilitated by the uniformity offered through a solitary church that took as a tenet of faith that the king ruled by God's grace. The state invoked its police power to criminalize individuals who undermined this ordered consciousness. Persons who worked for the state as judges, prosecutors and police facilitated the government objective of rule through intimidating use of police power. The circuit breaker in this use of criminal law was the people sitting as jury and holding the capacity out of sheer conscience to simply not invoke the law regardless of the absence of factual contention and the clarity of the judge's instructions. The professionals all resisted the jury recognizing the extent of its power, but the jury, when the facts of the case called to their emotions, proved able to resist the judicial order. Then as now, when government uses prosecution to control social change, they risk an undesired result if the people are empowered with the final say.

A strikingly similar lesson is related in the 1735 prosecution of John Peter Zenger. Zenger, printer of a newspaper in New York colony, published a letter critical of the Governor and so was prosecuted for the crime of seditious libel. Such prosecution makes eminent sense when the purpose of criminal law is recognized as the upholding of ruling order against the challenge of disobedience. The court cooperated with the state and admonished the jury that they could not consider the truth of the published statements because truth was not legally accepted as a defense against the crime of criticizing government. The judge instructed that the only task for the jury was to determine if Zenger was the publisher and if the comments were critical. The judge insisted that if the jury found obviously true determinations, then they must find Zenger guilty and turn him over to the court for punishment.

Andrew Hamilton invoked the defense employed by Penn. He asked the jury to place the law on trial and to use their own ideas of morality rather than the government's instructions as a guide. He eloquently asked the jury to define their job in grand terms:

> The question before the Court and you gentlemen of the jury is not of small nor private concern, it is not the cause of a small printer, nor of New York alone, which you are

> now trying: No! It may in its consequence affect every freeman that lives under a British government on the main of America. It is the best cause. It is the cause of liberty; and I make no doubt that but your upright conduct this day will not only entitle you to the love and estime of your fellow citizens; but every man who prefers freedom to a life of slavery will bless and honor you as men who have baffled the attempt of tyranny; and by an impartial and uncorrupt verdict, have laid a noble foundation for securing to ourselves, our posterity and our neighbors that to which nature and the laws of our country have given us as right—the liberty—both of exposing and opposing arbitrary power by speaking and writing truth.

The jury rose to the charge and, in disregard of the commands of the judge, delivered a verdict of not guilty.[3]

When the British government became more serious about using the criminal justice system to force submission, the necessary next step was to eliminate the role of the jury. This path was taken in the Stamp Act confrontation. This denial of the right of jury authority as a means to bolster control of society through prosecution helps to explain the insistence on the jury prerogative in the subsequent constitutional text.

One instance of Stamp Act confrontation involved the suspected smuggler John Hancock. Failure to pay the stamp tax to the British was a criminal act, undermining the public economy and challenging the sovereignty of the state. In one smuggling case the government contended,

> It is true the common privileges of Englishmen are taken away in this Case, but even their privileges are not so in cases of Crime and fine. Tis the necessity of the Case and the benefit of the Revenue that justifies the Writ. Is not the Revenue the sole support of Fleets and Armies abroad, and Ministers at home? Without which the Nation could neither be preserved from Invasions of her foes, nor the Tumults of her own Subjects.

With reasoning such as this it seemed proper to deny jury trials to smuggling defendants, as such rights only impeded the police authority to gain profit for the state from commerce and to keep the people obedient through certain punishment to the sovereign power of the state.

Opinion within the public tended toward a different logic. Failure to pay the stamp tax lowered prices to the consumer and so was popular just as resistance to such "taxation without representation" emerged as a political movement. Given this public sentiment the royal government correctly perceived that jury trials were not in their interest. Demonstration of the importance of the presence or omission of the jury occurred in the prosecution of John Hancock. First he was tried in the courts of admiralty without a jury. Naturally the government's court found him guilty and seized his ship and assets. He then sued the customs officials in civil court for trespass on his ship. At this trial the judge ordered the jury not to question the decision of the admiralty court, an order they discarded to award the convicted smuggler damages. The message is quite clear: when the principle of the jury is upheld, political prosecution as a means of coercion is greatly limited for government.

The Declaration of Independence in its list of grievances against British rule stated that the king deprived us of the "benefit of trial by jury." In revolutionary political theory the importance of trial by jury grew. As Jeffery Abramson writes, local juries became the essential means by which democracy was practiced. Juries were seen as the best assurance that law and justice accurately reflected "the morals, values and common sense of the people."[4]

Thomas Jefferson wrote, "were I called upon to decide, whether the people had best be omitted in the legislative or judiciary department, I would say it is better to leave them out of the legislative. The execution of the law is more important than the making them."[5]

When the text of the Constitution was reported out of the Philadelphia convention, absence of an explicit promise for trial by jury was one of the concerns expressed in the ratification process. Six states formally called for addition of the right. Virginia and North Carolina jointly called for recognition of "trial by an impartial Jury" as a defendant's right. And so the right was formalized in the text of the Sixth Amendment.

In emphasizing jury trial, Americans were in part reflecting an historic element of British law, mixed with awareness that oppressive government by necessity violated this rule. They were affirming a traditional right based on an experience of breach of that right. Years later the Supreme Court wrote that the purpose of the jury was "to prevent oppression by Government" and to infuse the law with "the common sense judgement of a group of laymen . . . representative of a cross section of the community."[6]

In reality this great legacy of trial by jury has little to do with most criminal law today except in the rare instance of wealthy criminal defendants. Government has decided to conduct a war on crime defined substantially as forbidden recreational activity such as illegal drug use and prostitution. The jury trial is not compatible with a policy of culturally motivated mass incarceration. Jury trials reflect an age in which people were free to conduct their own affairs and in which criminal justice prided itself on hearings devoted to consideration of the individual. As the will to remold American culture through mass prosecution has shifted the mission of the police, jury trials came to be seen as an unnecessary expense and an interference with the efficiency of mass incarceration. Some 2 percent of arrests culminate today in jury deliberations. Ninety percent of persons incarcerated receive no trial at all. Eighty percent of persons who suffer forfeiture of their property are never even charged with a criminal act. For most victims of the criminal justice system, administrative discretion and plea bargaining is the extent of process granted by the state. State-appointed defense attorneys and public prosecutors simply must cooperate to induce defendants to accept conviction without constitutional process in order to dispose of the flow of humanity dumped upon them. Constitutional criminal procedure is not compatible with wholesale criminalization. If the individual were considered as a single case by a jury, then many demands for incarceration would be rejected. What is the legitimate purpose to sending a person to prison for decades because his vices are unfashionable? How in good conscience can the defendant be held guilty beyond a reasonable doubt when the police are corrupt, racist and in a state of declared war with the community? Only by dehumanizing the process can such will to mass punishment be sustained. Finally, as the state demands the criminalization of the majority of the male youth of some minority group, the state cannot count on the cooperation of the adults in that community to obediently serve the state and legitimate the race-based mass incarceration. And so as the racial aspect of the drug war became more clear, government has felt compelled to find means to eliminate the jury system in our day.

This criticism is similarly well directed at the institution of the grand jury. The Fifth Amendment states that "no person shall be answerable for a capital, or otherwise infamous crime, unless on a presentment of a Grand Jury. . . ." Before the state was permitted to subject a person to the expense and burden of a criminal action, the people meeting in a preliminary jury capacity were asked for consent. The grand jury was meant to be another among many protections against a powerful police state. Like the other tenets of the Constitutional criminal model, the reality is a mockery of the promise. Today grand juries function largely as the investigative and indictment rubber stamp of the prosecutorial office. The decision to prosecute is no longer a matter controlled by the people; the grand jury serves as a dumb and silent legitimating force providing the form of Constitutionalism while precluding the substance. Should any grand jury begin to recognize its public trust and obligation to critically say no to officials, it is summarily dismissed to be replaced by a prosecution-friendly group. The criminal justice system is simply too busy, with over a million drug charges alone per year, to accept the quaint eccentricities of Constitutional justice.

The Fourth Amendment continues this story of noble historic promise and contemporary breach. In the era of true monarchy respect for the home and privacy of the individual fell outside the ideas of jurisprudence, political philosophy and theology. The state and church were locked in a struggle on the side of God and in opposition to chaos, disobedience, crime and Satan. Any notion of privacy was simply a tool to hide the enemy. The state had to be all powerful to do king and God's will on a corrupted rebellious earth.

As one example of this absolute license to ferret out deviance, the recusancy laws of 1606 directed searches in "the Howses and Lodgings of every convicted Popishe Recusant."[7] The Court of High Commission extended these rules to include all persons so to guarantee the absence of religious dissent. Directives from the Privy Council similarly authorized a search for evidence of political unrest.

As the Enlightenment began to ponder ideas of liberty and nonconformity, the idea of privacy emerged and began to transform the law. The judicial victory of John Wilkes highlights this transformation. In 1763 Wilkes and 48 others were arrested. His house was searched for his personal papers, and he was charged with seditious libel. The court sided with his view that the entering of his house constituted trespass. The judge wrote, "to enter a man's house by virtue of a nameless warrant . . . is worse than the Spanish Inquisition; a law under which no Englishman could live for an hour."[8]

William Pitt is credited with the most eloquent statement of the emerging liberal sentiment as he argued for abolition of the principle of general warrants. "The poorest man may, in his cottage, bid defiance to all the forces of the crown. It may be frail; its roof may shake; the wind may blow through it; the storm may enter; the rain may enter, but the King of England may not enter; all his force dares not cross the threshold of the ruined tenement."[9]

As with trial by jury, the royal government found the emerging idea of limit to the police search power inconvenient. Also in parallel to the history of the right to jury trial, the colonials found denial of privacy an offense that became a revolutionary rallying cry. The Writs of Assistance case is a famous instance of British denial of criminal justice rights leading to pre-revolutionary discontent. In this case customs officials were given the authority to enter boats that were also domicile to the crew to search for untaxed imports. The defense argued that such general writs violated British law. The juryless court found the writs legal. John Adams remarked 60 years later, "then and there the child of independence was born."

Based on this type of experience the subsequent state constitutions called for guarantees against police prerogative to conduct searches. The Virginia Declaration of Rights labeled searches of "suspected places without evidence of a fact committed, or to seize any person or persons not named, or whose offense is not particularly described and supported by evidence, are grievous and oppressive, and ought not to be granted." The Massachusetts Constitution promised that "Every subject has a right to be secure from all unreasonable searches and seizures," and that all "warrants therefore are contrary to this right if the cause or foundation of them be not previously supported by oath or affirmation."

As with trial by jury, the absence in the draft of the federal Constitution of a guaranteed right against oppressive searches became a rallying cry. This sentiment was specifically expressed in the ratification proceedings of New York, North Carolina and Virginia. And so the Fourth Amendment promise represents a continuation of prior heritage and revolutionary commitment.

Also in parallel to the right to trial by jury, the Fourth Amendment has been violated beyond recognition in the modern demand for police authority to cure society of bad values. Schoolchildren in disregard of the heritage and promise can be forced to urinate in search for evidence of forbidden drugs. Helicopters can fly over citizens' homes and property searching for wicked plants. Cars, boats and planes are stopped and searched without warrant. The next chapter will review how the politically appointed Supreme Court reigned over the abandonment of this promised limit on police authority.

The Eighth Amendment prohibition against "excessive fines" or "cruel and unusual punishment" has also proven worthless in the face of modern will for punitive domestic crusade. A portion of the sad irony of this particular breach of the Constitutional promise is provided by recognition that though it is substantially in the name of religious-inspired zeal for punishment of sin that the Constitutional criminal justice promises have been voided, the origins of the Eighth Amendment have a contradictory religious origin. A portion of the Eighth Amendment heritage has to do with proportionality, the idea that a punishment should no more than fit a crime. Here the biblical injunction of no more than the value of an eye for an eye or a tooth for a tooth is relevant. Where is the proportionality in the sale of a personal use quantity of marijuana warranting 20 years or more in prison?

As with other aspects of the civil liberties tradition, the Magna Carta presents an important step in the evolution of this right. Chapter Fourteen promised that punishment would not be excessive, in particular that freemen would not lose their status for trivial offenses. Freedom from excessive punishment was repeated in 1689 as a right in the Bill of Rights proclaimed by William and Mary.

Following in this tradition, 9 states included limitation in punishment in their state constitutions. The Pennsylvania Constitution called for all fines to be "moderate." Thomas Jefferson instructed "Let mercy be the characteristic of the lawgiver."[10]

Before the Bill of Rights was ratified the prohibition against cruel and unusual punishment was included by Congress in the Northwest Ordinance as a government principal for the territories. Objection to the absence of this right was heard in many ratification forums, including a stirring speech by Patrick Henry in Virginia. He argued that torture was the tool of governments when it is not forbidden.

In disregard of all this, massive sentencing for vice crimes, confining citizens to horrendous prisons for decades is the norm of the American republic today. In 1980 the United States Supreme Court upheld a sentence of life imprisonment for a man who had 3 theft offenses that totaled less than $230.[11] In another case the Supreme Court upheld a conviction of 20 years for a person found in possession of less than an ounce of marijuana.[12]

A topic of importance throughout the revolutionary and Constitutional experience was the oppressiveness of government when rulers kept standing armed forces to control the people. At the Philadelphia Constitutional Convention there was repeated discussion of the danger of allowing government to raise standing armies in time of peace. Mr. Gerry pointed out that "great opposition to the plan would spring from" the omission of a limit on the raising of standing forces.[13]

This sentiment, ultimately transformed into the Constitutional injunction against military appropriations spanning over 2 years and the Second Amendment, springs from a long political experience. In feudal England the right to bear arms was dictated by status. According to one law no person who had not land of a yearly value of £100, or an heir of an esquire or other persons of high degree, was allowed to keep a gun. Landed proprietors were required to have in readiness specific arms and equipment and trained men kept at their expense for use of the state when called into service. At the time of the restoration of the monarchy in the person of Charles II, no other armed force was recognized as lawful. Hence the distribution and limitation of arms under law stabilized a political order for the benefit of the gentry.

Charles II and more so his successor James II attempted to shift the balance of domestic rule by building a central army loyal to the crown. This force was meant to undermine the independent power away from the local gentry. The Declaration of Rights proclaimed by the Convention Parliament after the forced abdication of James, denounced the building of an armed force as an "endeavor to subvert" the "laws and liberties of this kingdom." The subsequent Bill of Rights directed "That the raising or keeping a standing army within the kingdom in time of peace unless it be with the consent of parliament is against the law."

And so when the colonists complained that the government resorted to the maintenance of armed forces among the people to preserve its reign, they were reflecting another traditional tension between a people and their rulers. The Declaration of Independence listed as one of the grievances that the king had kept a standing army among the people in time of peace. The need to maintain rule by force of arms was seen as proof of bad government.

Many of the state constitutions reflected the idea that when the government holds men-at-arms in the state it fundamentally changes the civilization away from republican principle to one of rulership and force. Hence the Virginia Constitution declared "A well-regulated militia composed of the body of the people is the proper, natural, and safe defense of a free state." The Pennsylvania Constitution of 1776 stated "as standing armies in the time of peace, are dangerous to liberty, they ought not to be kept up."

As modern America declared war on the behavior of its own people, the need to keep armed standing police forces in the states and cities has grown. The first national police force, the Federal Bureau of Investigation, was not founded until the federal government declared Prohibition. The War on Drugs vastly increased the importance of federal police authority. In Los Angeles, under the leadership of Police Chief Gates, tanks were used as battering rams to prosecute the War on Drugs by leveling the homes of suspected users and sellers. In New York, under the leadership of Mayor Koch, whole apartment houses were leveled, with the justification that if people were allowed to live in them drug dealing would occur. In instances throughout the nation the police have become an occupying force charged with controlling the undesired local inhabitants. In Texas the marines patrol as police agents to combat the drug trade. Again the fundamental covenant of the American civilization has been abandoned to unwise and unworkable police policies.

Another Constitutional promise meant to limit oppressive use of the police power is the Sixth Amendment guarantee of the right to defense counsel. The state-appointed defense counsel system meant to provide a meaningful fulfillment of this pledge, has turned into a mockery of it. Public defenders offices, whatever their intention, because of case loads and budgets are, in fact, a portion of the bureaucratic apparatus that causes virtually all the young and poor defendants to plead guilty rather than mount a Constitutionally guaranteed jury trial. A consequence of the declarations of wars on drugs, pornography and crime is that private defense attorneys have come to be treated as traitors to the prosecuting national order.

Habeas Corpus is another of the long list of rights that evolved with Western civilization, was recognized in the text of the Constitution, and has become politically unpopular in this age of popularized punishment. Often referred to as "The Great Writ of Liberty," Habeas Corpus is one of the few procedural rights written into the Philadelphia text. This right, to be brought before a court to have incarceration justified, was seen as a basic tool to keep the armed power of the state in check. Only in time of extreme national duress has this right been questioned. Most famously during the Civil War, military authorities claimed the power to hold rebels without judicial supervision. With no real national emergency as justification, the right of appearance before a judicial tribunal that employs Constitutional procedures is seen as too expensive for this mass incarceration age.

Even the First Amendment, not usually thought of as one of the criminal justice provisions and often referred to as the essence of the Constitutional promise, has been compromised in the modern will for mass criminalization. The Virginia Declaration of Rights read, "That the freedom of the Press is one of the greatest bulwarks of liberty and can never be restrained but by despotic Governments." The Pennsylvania Constitution stated, "That the people have a right to freedom of speech, and of writing and publishing their sentiments; therefore the freedom of the press ought not to be restrained." Madison's proposed draft of the Bill of Rights before Congress read, "the people shall not be deprived or abridged of their right to speak, to write or to publish their sentiments; and the freedom of the press, as one of the great bulwarks of liberty, shall be inviolable." Few sentiments were as broadly held and respected among citizens in the founding generation; 9 of the 11 state constitutions expressed such sentiment.

In this age of punishment a new forum for conversation among the people emerged. Not much time passed between the success of the Internet and demand heard in Congress and the body politic for the criminalization of illicit conversations that transpire within it. With the release of a study claiming that a third of Internet use was sexually motivated, a new rallying emerged for yet another attempt to find salvation for maligned culture through mass incarceration. Discovery that the research that produced this report was ideologically driven and empirically false and deceitful did little to diminish the zeal for new laws and new punishment. As so often in modern politics, human behavior thought by some to be sinful is quickly transformed into criminal. The lack of fair research into the public policy consequences of the sinful behavior or measurable benefit of the new incarceration does not diminish the demand for punishment which is itself cultural and so not concerned with issues of rational objectivity. The Constitutional prohibition of the use of police power to suppress speech did not deter the proponents of punishment. Unusually, in this instance the Supreme Court did invoke and uphold the First Amendment. The next chapter will detail how rare such behavior by the judiciary has been in contemporary constitutional criminal law.

Many of the remaining elements of the Constitution related to criminal justice involve large questions such as: In a government of 3 co-equal branches what is the province of the judiciary and when do laws forbidding judicial discretion deprive the Courts of the responsibility for individual case determination? The California State Supreme Court grappled with this question in their rejection of the aspect of the Three Strikes laws that gave the executive the ability to consider the individual in applying punishment but denied such discretion to the judicial branch. A related question is raised in consideration of the meaning of the fundamental Constitutional promise of due process. When do laws that deny the individual the ability to have his case heard as a personal matter deny that individual due process of law?

The phrase "due process of law" is drawn from a 1345 act of Parliament reconfirming Magna Carta while changing the older promise of justice "by the law of the land" to the new "due process" term. The change in language paralleled the increasing importance and complexity of common law. When the royal Star Chamber and Courts of High Commission were abolished by Parliament in 1641, the legacy of due process was cited as the proof of wrongness of such executive tribunals. Due process is at the heart of the argument for an independent judiciary.

The rise of the autonomous judiciary is synonymous with and causative of the movement toward liberty. As late as 1607 an angry Archbishop Bancroft rebuked Chief Justice Coke that "judges are but lions under the throne" and as such must in all ways be subservient to the king and his will to use law to punish opposition. The king added weight to the lesson by threatening the chief justice with his sword if he continued to resist the king's will to incarcerate a rebellious barrister. Coke fell to his knees and was spared for having dared claim that the judicial process should be respected as outside royal hegemony. Since then, as the rule of crown and church fell, the autonomy and authority of the bench rose. By 1687 in the case of Seven Bishops, King James II accepted that even the monarch could punish his own clergy only through judicial process.

The Declaration of Independence made a point of the insult to human rights when government interfered in the province of the judiciary. Included in the list of grievances is the complaint that the king "has made judges dependant on his will alone" and that "he has obstructed the administration of justice." Every state that established a constitution constructed an independent judiciary to order justice and preserve liberty.

At the constitutional convention all the models discussed for the new government included provision for a national judiciary. The Constitution ultimately created the federal judiciary as a co-equal branch of government, deriving its power from Article 3, as the legislative and executive branches are each constructed by the first two. Of the judiciary Alexander Hamilton wrote that it is

> requisite to guard the Constitution and the rights of the individuals from the effects of those ill humors which the art of designing men, or the influence of particular conjunctures, sometime disseminate among the people themselves, and which, though they speedily give place to better information, and more deliberate reflection, have a tendency, in the meantime, to occasion dangerous innovations in the government, and serious oppressions of the minor party in the community.[14]

In 1996 Judge Baer, Jr. dared to live up to the Constitutionally appointed task of standing against the "ill humor" of our age. He ruled against the admissibility as evidence of drugs seized by New York police. Senior politicians from both political parties made this an opportunity to again proclaim their disinterest in permitting Constitutional values to interfere in the domestic war. President Clinton, who had appointed the judge to the Federal District Court, stated that if the judge did not reverse his ruling then he would call for resignation. The Republican presidential nominee Bob Dole and Speaker of the House Newt Gingrich went further and called for impeachment. Under this political pressure the judge reversed his ruling. As usual, in time of domestic crusade the supposedly neutral branch is called upon to legitimate government authority rather than opposing it by demanding the rule of law. The chief judge of the Second Circuit labeled the political pressure as "extraordinary intimidation."[15]

Chapter Three of this book turns to the question of how the Supreme Court has abandoned its Constitutionally appointed role as guardian of the people's liberties against police power. A fear in society in this age of popularized punishment is that the Constitutional model will work and the courts will act as guardians of constitutional values, dispensing liberty and unoppressive justice in defiance of the "ill humor" that demands mass incarceration. And so laws are passed to strip the courts of the ability to provide due process and consider the case of an individual. To achieve assembly line punishment such vengeful laws as mandatory sentencing and the various three strikes initiatives were constructed. At base all such laws are antijudicial. These laws are designed to prevent courts from hearing an individual's case and ruling with a justice that has the potential of mercy or moral complexity.

Some judges have rebelled against this preclusion of due process. Fifty of the 680 federal judges refuse to hear any drug cases because of the cruel sentencing guidelines. The judicial councils of all twelve federal circuits passed resolutions in 1990 and 1991 asking Congress to reconsider federal mandatory sentencing laws. As society has decided that it must criminalize a significant share of its whole population, the individualism promised by due process and inherent in the provence of the judiciary has been replaced by an assembly line, except for those who can through personal resources purchase the Constitutional process that should be the right of all.

The great addition to the national commitment to liberty after the Bill of Rights is the promise subsequent to the Civil War of equal protection. It has been especially violated in the will for mass incarceration. Two-thirds of black males under the age of 30 will be arrested. A third of these are now under control of the criminal justice system, either as prisoner or on parole. Statistically, blacks constitute 12 percent of the population, 13 percent of the drug users and yet receive 35 percent of the drug use arrests, 55 percent of the convictions and serve 75 percent of the incarceration time. Every aspect of the criminal justice system works to oppress the underprivileged, the opposite of the dream of a more equal society. One in 7 black males, one and a half million persons, is barred from voting due to felony conviction or status in prison or parole. Between 1986 and 1991 the number of blacks imprisoned for drugs increased 465 percent.[16]

Both whites and blacks seek chemical intoxication in large numbers. The will to get high is a fact of the human condition not significantly affected by race. Yet the primarily white drug of cocaine is punished at one level, admittedly excessive, while the predominantly black drug, crack, carries a much longer sentence, despite the fact that the active ingredient of crack is cocaine. The cheaper diluted version is punished more severely than the expensive real thing! This is one factor leading to the modern event of an 8 times greater likelihood of a black male serving prison time than a white male. With a third the young black males going to prison rather than to high school and college, equal protection is as illusory today as during the age of official segregation.

How has the Supreme Court, whose job it is to uphold the Constitution, allowed the nation to fall to this shabby state of justice? The answer is partly the fact that the public has demanded they do so. Further, this Supreme Court has been substantially selected for its loyalty to mass criminalization. Finally, over its history the Supreme Court has not proven to be committed to the criminal justice provisions of the Constitution. Chapter Three turns to the successful deployment of the Supreme Court with the mission of legitimating domestic warfare in betrayal of the array of contradictory Constitutional promises. The Constitution in practice is very different in the field of criminal justice from the Constitution as written.

NOTES

1. Paul Murphy, ed. *The Bill of Rights and American Legal History* (New York and London, Garland, 1990).
2. Ibid.
3. Stephen Presser and Jamil Zainaldin, *Law and Jurisprudence in American History* (St. Paul, West, 1995).
4. Jeffrey Abramson, *We, the Jury* (New York, Basic Books, 1994), p. 28.
5. Ibid.
6. *Apodaca v. Oregon*, 406 U.S. 404 (1972) at 409.
7. "The Origins of the Fourth Amendment," William Cuddihy, *William and Mary Quarterly*, Vol. 37, 1980, p. 371.
8. Ibid., p. 385.
9. David M. O'Brien, *Privacy, Law and Public Policy* (New York, Praeger, 1979), p. 28.
10. T. J. to Edmund Pendleton, 26 Aug. 1776, in Michael Kammen, *The Origins of the American Constitution* (New York, Penguin Books, 1986).
11. *Rummel v. Estelle*, 445 U.S. 263 (1980).
12. *Hutto v. Davis*, 454 U.S. 370 (1981).
13. James Madison, *Notes of Debate in the the Federal Convention of 1787* (New York, W. W. Norton, 1987), p. 48.
14. Federalist Papers, #78, Alexander Hamilton, James Madison and John Jay, *The Federalist Papers* (New York, Bantam Books, 1982).
15. "The Pressure on Baer," *Washington Post Weekly Magazine*, April 22, 1966.
16. *Drug Policy Newsletter*, Number 28, Winter 1996.

3

The Supreme Court, Constitutional Law and the War on Drugs

Constitutional criminal process has gone through multiple revolutions in the nation's experience. These revolutions in the rights of citizens in confrontation with the state have reflected the many changes in the mission of criminal justice, particularly the fluctuating levels of cultural conflict waged through the criminal justice system. Thus when immigrants were widely perceived as a problem by rural protestants in the early 1900s the nation responded with an array of criminal laws meant to reaffirm traditional culture.[1] Most famous of these is of course Prohibition, which successfully criminalized immigrant Italian, Irish Catholic and German workers for their recreational libations. Similarly laws forbidding lotteries, other forms of gambling, opium, marijuana and nonprocreational sexual activity helped the dominant community to declare the undesirables as unrighteous and criminal.

With these criminalization measures, the procedural rights of Americans were relaxed to aid the police in their work. As the various forms of sin are criminalized, procedural rights are perceived to be unwieldy. Cultural crimes by their victimless nature inspire combative and creative police conduct. Lacking a victim to make the accusation and provide information, crimes against culture require the police to greatly expand their arsenal of techniques. When the public wants the focus of criminal justice to be cultural warfare Constitutional rights are dismissed.

The case of *Olmstead v. United States* serves as a reminder of how the criminalization of cultural behavior translates into reduction of rights.[2] In that case the Supreme Court upheld the conviction of alcohol beverage importers based on wiretapped phone conversations. As usual in cases involving crimes against cultural practices, there were no cooperative victims or witnesses willing to provide testimony. If they are to be effective, police become compelled in enforcing cultural laws to adopt the very aggressive police measures forbidden in the Constitution.

In a manner that this chapter will show to be normal, the Court reached the astounding conclusion that the wiretapping of private conversations without a warrant by the police does not violate the Fourth Amendment prohibition against unreasonable searches and seizures. The basic justification the Court issued for so truncating individual liberty is the great scale of breach of national Prohibition laws. Articulating the ideology of social conservatism, the Court reasoned that the very failure of punitive law is justification to reject civil liberty and never cause to question the mission of police acting as domestic soldiers of moralist public policy. The Court goes on to explain that a search conducted by listening devices cannot be considered a prohibited search within the meaning of the Constitution because there is no physical entry. Such a ruling allows changes in technology to eliminate the values in the Constitutional text. That result is the opposite of the mission assigned to the judiciary of keeping the Constitution relevant. Instead the Court applies its power of interpretation to absolve the police from abandonment of Constitutional limits. The majority concluded that if they held government to "nice ethical conduct," then the result would be to "give criminals greater immunity."[3]

The majority opinion shows the capacity of the Court to subordinate Constitutional rights to the punitive policies of the day. The dissenting opinions by Justices Brandeis and Holmes demonstrate the alterative recessive capacity to take rights seriously. In what became one of the most quoted and farsighted dissenting opinions in the history of the Constitution Brandeis wrote,

> the makers of our Constitution undertook to secure conditions favorable to the pursuit of happiness. They recognized the significance of man's spiritual nature, of his feelings and of his intellect. They knew that only a part of the pain, pleasure and satisfactions of life are found in material things. They sought to protect Americans in their beliefs, their thoughts, their emotions and their sensations. They conferred, as against the Government, the right to be let alone—the most comprehensive of rights and the right most valued by civilized men. To protect that right, every unjustified intrusion by the Government upon the privacy of the individual, whatever the means employed, must be deemed a violation of the Fourth Amendment.

Brandeis concluded his remarks by warning that,

> Our Government is the potent, the omnipresent teacher. For good or for ill, it teaches the whole people by its example. Crime is contagious. If the Government becomes a lawbreaker, it breeds contempt for the law; it invites every man to become a law unto himself; it invites anarchy. To declare that in the administration of the criminal law the end justifies the means—to declare that the Government may commit crimes in order to secure the conviction of a private criminal—would bring terrible retribution.[4]

Brandeis recognized the strong tendency to use criminal law to achieve cultural objectives. He declared that the Constitution forbids this end. He warned that for a government to be good it first must follow the fundamental laws that limit its conduct; it must learn to leave its people alone.

Despite the warnings of these justices, government in their day conducted a sweeping cultural crusade that targeted immigrant men by criminalization of alcohol, their recreational drug of choice. Criminalization of lotteries, gambling, drugs and sexual commerce were similar attempts to preserve a purified image of the traditional dominant culture against undesired change. In all these instances the Court only facilitated the expansion of police mission and authority despite contradictory constitutional text.

The majority view, that criminal law is appropriately used to guard traditional cultural order and never should be deterred in this task by the Constitutional promise of rights, reached its logical conclusion in the judicially endorsed interment of Japanese during World War II. The due process clause and equal protection clause ought to have comprehensively forbidden the policy that a race can be declared criminal without individual consideration of the question of participation in subversion. As during the War on Drugs and the confinement of protestors during World War I, fear and hate combined with the high court's mission supportive reading of the Constitution to facilitate and legitimate applied police rule.

The criminalization of advocates for social change in the McCarthy era marks the beginning of the great reversal in judicial behavior. Advocates of the poor and of workers' rights had entered the mainstream of American culture since the New Deal. In the era of understandable fear surrounding Soviet expansion, they became targets of a cultural rampage funneled into police authority. At first hesitantly, then with greater resolve, the Court for the first time questioned the use of such government power to control social change. Starting with *Yates v. United States*, the Court began to give stricter scrutiny to the political use of criminal law.[5] This will to limit the use of police power when employed as a mechanism of social and political control became a focus of the docket expressed in such cases as *Watkins v. United States* which limited the search for communists, *NAACP v. Alabama*, which limited the search for civil rights activists, and *Brandenburg v. Ohio*, which limited prosecution for other forms of political activism, in this instance advocacy of racism under the Klu Klux Klan banner.

This substantive limitation on the use of police power as a means of enforcing tradition and social order reached its zenith in the case *Griswold v. Connecticut*.[6] Traditional order included preservation of religiously inspired gender roles. By these roles sex was only permitted when performed between husband and wife for the purpose of procreation. Substantial portions of the criminal code were devoted to maintaining this social order. Conservative ideology then and now regarded the traditional family as the key to promotion of traditional social order. Hence adultery, abortion, fornication, homosexuality and contraception use were all crimes. These laws enforced a religious propriety and encouraged traditional family roles. In striking the laws criminalizing the use or sale of contraception the Court found in the Constitution a "zone of privacy" that limited the substantive range of police authority. A series of subsequent cases, particularly *Roe v. Wade*[7] and *Stanley v. Georgia*,[8] placed many of the traditional sexual crimes outside the boundaries of criminal law. As moralists feared and warned, American culture did, in fact, significantly change as police were withdrawn from this portion of cultural enforcement. The sexual revolution with its many ramifications was a direct product of these judicial decrees among other sources.

This will to find liberty interests in the Constitution found expression in an array of procedural reforms and constitutes the only period in American history when the promises forbidding prohibited police power achieved significant enforcement. *Mapp v. Ohio* is one of many cases highlighting the differences between the Warren Court era treatment and other periods.[9] The defendant was convicted and tried for the cultural crime of possession of pornography. The pictures and books were seized "during an unlawful search of the defendants home." The police broke into the defendants home, falsely claimed to have a search warrant, and treated her with brutality. Most courts would have found a way to justify this abusive use of police power in order to uphold the authority of the state. The state's attorney, in fact, argued that the illegality of the police behavior should not bar criminalization of the defendant for possession of forbidden pictures.

The Supreme Court in this case disagreed and asserted that there is in the Fourth Amendment a Constitutional right of privacy that is enforceable against state police behavior through the due process clause of the Fourteenth Amendment.

In contrast to most of Constitutional history, the expressed concern of the Court in this case is not that the state enforce tradition and authority by controlling undesired culture, but rather that the government live up to the charter of liberty and so allow a diversity of cultures and expressions to flourish. The majority opinion states, "Our decision, founded on reason and truth, gives to the individual no more than that which the Constitution guarantees him, to the police officer no less than that to which honest law enforcement is entitled, and to the courts, that judicial integrity so necessary in the true administration of justice."[10]

This willingness to serve as fair enforcer of the Constitutional guarantees of liberty rather than pro-government partisan in a cultural struggle was again exhibited in the case of *Katz v. United States*.[11] In that case the Court considered the validity of evidence obtained by bugging a public telephone booth. The evidence showed that the defendant was engaged in the then culturally offensive practice of gambling. The Court acknowledged the centrality of the Fourth Amendment to the quality of liberty by stating the clause "protects people—and not simply areas—against unreasonable searches and seizures."

In an array of other cases the Court limited abuse in the criminal justice process and misuse of police power. Most significant cases in this era include *Gideon v. Wainwright*, in which the Court ruled that if the state subjects an indigent person to the pain of prosecution, it must afford him competent legal council, and *Miranda v. Arizona* which outlined the rules police must follow respecting an individual's rights once taken into custody.

With the launching of the War on Drugs and other criminalization offensives in the 1980s and 1990s, the rights written into the text and implemented by the Court during the prior decades became a target. The judiciary as a whole came under attack as "soft on crime" and for creating rights. By the end of the Bush administration every one of the justices who had participated in the revival of Constitutional criminal rights was replaced. The new justices implemented a sweeping abandonment of the limits on police abuse. By the mid-1990s the Fourth, Fifth, Sixth and Eighth Amendments were effectively eliminated from the reality of criminal justice operations, thus allowing the nation's greatest police assault on bad culture to be conducted under the names "War on Drugs," "War on Pornography" and "War on Crime." As before, when conservative culture became threatened, it responded by criminalization of those behaviors found to be sinful and deviant. Constitutional rights again became a barrier to the waging of successful cultural warfare. That barrier is demolished.

In 1990 Chief Justice Rehnquist announced that the job of the judiciary was to support the war effort by ensuring that large numbers of Americans were successfully prosecuted and incarcerated. He pleaded to Congress to create large numbers of new district courts so the federal bench would not get behind in its conviction productivity. He warned "The War on Drugs will fail if the judiciary is not given the judgeships necessary to do the job."[12] Absent from his comments or subsequent behavior was any idea that the courts should see themselves as guarantors of constitutional values or even as simple neutral referees.

John Decker's book, *Revolution to the Right: Criminal Procedure Jurisprudence During the Burger-Rehnquist Court Era*, attempts to explain the means by which the modern court has used its institutional authority to legitimate abandonment of the Constitution in police affairs.[13] The author explains that starting in the 1968 election, President Nixon made the Supreme Court a target, launching his greatest rhetorical fire on the extension of Constitutional rights to police affairs. Conservatives through Reagan and Bush followed this example and seated a Supreme Court that viewed the declaration of guilt rather than the protection of rights to be the work product of the judiciary. The author asserted that the modern court makes "symbolic gestures" by reciting the text and history of the amendments, while undermining the plain values and meaning of the Constitution in practice.

Modern jurisprudence runs on a model that seeks to legitimate police authority while not actually limiting police conduct. First the Court invokes the text of the Constitution and recites the history and values of the civil liberties tradition in laudatory terms. This is followed in the case text with recitation of all the advantages this defendant has already enjoyed under the bountiful liberty of the Constitution. Thus the court paints "a picture that the defendant has already had his day in court, maybe too many days."[14] Finally the Court shows how despite the promise of broad protection, the defendant in this case is entitled to no relief at all. When all the exceptions the Court has announced over the years to the Amendments are considered, there turns out to be little and sometimes no Constitutional promise left.

A case review of the ejection of Constitutional rights from the criminal justice system is essential to understanding the political success and moral failure of the modern cultural war. There exist now a wealth of cases that individually and in sum show the rule of law to be abandoned to a domestic war sociology. Sixty-two percent of the polled public in 1989 said that they would "give up some of their freedoms" to combat drug use.[15] They got their way in abundance.

Perhaps the case that most explicitly declares that the nation's drug warriors have permission to operate without restraint from law is *United States v. Alvarez-Machain*.[16] The Court is asked to consider whether federal agents can kidnap a foreign national on foreign soil in abrogation of international law and in clear violation of territorial integrity and in violation of the valid extradition treaty. Shockingly the Court states that they can. Cynically they attempt a word game to obfuscate this outrageous declaration.

Mexico demanded the return of its citizen, Alvarez-Machain, charged in the United States with participation in the slaying of a drug enforcement agent working in Mexico and was rebuffed by the federal government. Had the positions stood reversed, the United States might well have considered the infraction by the other nation to be an act of war. In dissent Justice Stevens wrote that the executive's interest in capturing this foreign national, "provides no justification for discarding the rule of law that this Court has a duty to uphold." Stevens warned that "The way that we perform that duty in a case of this kind sets an example that other tribunals in other countries are sure to emulate."[17]

So on the international scene, the Court gave a gloss of propriety to what is in truth raw terrorist behavior by the government and so weakens the rule of law. Chief Justice Rehnquist attempts the fig leaf rationalization that even though there is an extradition treaty, nothing in that treaty actually states that each nation will not cross the border and kidnap the other's citizens. Under the chief's leadership the Court furthered the objectives of dirty police work at the expense of the rule of law. The Mexican government in the following years understandably refused further cooperation with America's drug policies.

In the domestic sphere the Fourth Amendment received similar deliberate belittlement. In this instance the Court has consistently denied the Amendment's promise of a right to be "left alone" so as to allow authoritarian police practices to go unhindered. One such example is provided in the case of *Florida v. Bostick*.[18] In that case armed police took to the practice of boarding buses en route to conduct searches among the passengers to find drug carriers. The Florida State Supreme Court recognized that the passenger in question was seized because the armed officers blocked the exit of a loaded bus and rendering leaving difficult or impossible.

The police submitted that the defendant agreed to have his bags searched, an assertion which he denies. The Supreme Court found not only that there was no coercion in this situation, but that the search, while lacking basis through suspicion, was consensual. To support the war effort they asserted the man simply voluntarily agreed to let police look in a bag which he knew to contain contraband.

Justice Marshall writing for the dissent surmised that "our nation we are told is engaged in a 'war on drugs.' No one will dispute that it is the job of law enforcement officials to devise effective weapons for fighting this war. But effectiveness of a law enforcement technique is not proof of its constitutionality." He recognized that the Court's rejection of his logic and embrace of this tactic "violates the core values of the Fourth Amendment."[19]

In a different case,[20] in which the Supreme Court upheld forced urine testing for customs agents, Justice Marshall wrote, "There is no drug exception to the Constitution." In one sense this assertion is clearly false, judicial loyalty to this domestic war has rewritten virtually all defendant rights. However, in a much different sense than the author intended, the assertion is true in that the entirety of Constitutional police restraint is diminished in conformity with the drug exception. America's culture war as supported by the Court has rewritten the Constitution for our era.

All this led Wisconsin to specifically write a drug war exception to the Fourth Amendment idea that the police needed to knock and announce themselves before executing a search warrant. The state in reading the prior cases assumed that police could simply break in.[21] The Court wrote that while it would decline to agree that drug cases were exempt from the Constitution as a matter of law, by application they agreed police could usually make unannounced forcible entries simply by showing that present circumstances indicate that the police might endanger themselves or risk loss of evidence if they acted in a less vigorous manner. The Court agreed most drug cases could meet that standard. Applying its own rhetoric the Court upheld the unannounced forced entry in the case under consideration even while denying the blunt language of the statute.

Respect for private property is one of the historic concerns of the Fourth Amendment and one of the expressed priorities of the sitting Supreme Court. Yet the Court diminished the rights of all property owners in the case *Oliver v. United States*. In this case, the owner of the property is instructed that even though he fenced his grounds, erected a gate, posted "no trespassing" signs and lived on the property, there was no Fourth Amendment right requiring the police to obtain a warrant before forcibly searching the grounds for marijuana. Empowering the police to fight this cultural war exceeded as a value the Court's fundamental commitment to property rights.

The three-justice dissent characterized the conclusion as shocking. Marshall wrote that it is the role of the Court "when interpreting these seminal constitutional provisions, to effectuate their purposes—to lend them meanings that ensure that the liberties the Framers sought to protect are not undermined by the changing activities of government officials." The dissent lectured the majority on the traditional tests used to find Fourth Amendment interest. These include whether the privacy interest is protected by law. In this instance trespass, as conducted by the police, is a traditional crime. Also whether the person expecting privacy "manifested that interest to the public in a way most people would understand and respect."[22] Clearly a private residence fenced and displaying "no trespassing" signs fulfilled this condition. Further undermining property rights, the Court has accepted the authority of police to fly low over private property in their warrantless search for forbidden plants. The drug exception undermines all Constitutional concerns and reveals the Court as simply implementing political policy preferences without regard to Constitutional values.

Given the willingness of the Court to sacrifice the privacy interests of home owners, it should be no surprise that car drivers have also found themselves excluded from the ever-shrinking Fourth Amendment promise. Three recent cases have created a rule that despite the Constitutional promise to the contrary police may stop and search a car and its sealed contents without first bothering with the traditional warrant requirement. In one of these cases Justice Marshall wrote that this decision is "contrary to sound elaboration of established Fourth Amendment principles."[23] Yet again the will of the Court to support domestic war prevailed. Not surprisingly all three cases involved forbidden drugs.

Personal clothing forms a natural continuation to the judicially imposed elimination of the Fourth Amendment. In *New Jersey v. T.L.O.* the Court upheld marijuana introduced as evidence of a teenager's forbidden vice taken by a school official who reached into the student's purse to search for suspected tobacco.[24] The seized marijuana was then used in juvenile delinquency hearings against the girl. A dissent points out that the teaching lesson of this case is to show schoolchildren that the Constitution is a sham.

Even the human body has been excluded from Fourth Amendment definition in deference to the domestic struggle. The Court has held that suspicionless forced blood and urine testing of transportation employees is Constitutional. As with all judicial behavior in the drug war context, the result of this case proved to be driven far more by public passion than anything approaching Constitutional scholarship. In 1987 Amtrak's Colonial train with 616 passengers aboard was traveling at 105 miles an hour when it plowed into a string of Conrail freight engines. Fifteen people were killed, and another 176 injured. Initial investigation showed that equipment failure led to the accident. Days after the accident the Federal Aviation Administration's forensic toxicology unit announced that tetrahydrocannabinol (THC) was found in the blood of two of the freight train's crew. This news took hold with the public and sparked an outcry for widespread testing of transportation workers. Months later the Federal Aviation Administration reassigned the researcher who performed the laboratory work. He pleaded guilty in federal court to falsifying blood results in this and other cases. The real question of this and so many other instances where drug-related harm proved to be fabricated is why the public is so anxious to believe the false data. The public's love of drug fear drives criminal justice policy and Constitutional law.

The Court has allowed the various police agencies to seize people with little or no basis. In *California v. Hodari* the Court accepted the constitutionality of police chasing youths with the only basis of suspicion that the kids fled when they saw the police approaching.[25] The Court did not characterize the chase as a seizure so that if cocaine was discarded, it could be submitted as evidence. Similarly in *Minnesota v. Dickerson*, a police officer was allowed to frisk a man on the basis of his leaving a 12-unit apartment building because one of the apartments was believed to be in the prohibited trade and because he turned and walked away from the police car.[26]

In the wake of such decisions police have felt empowered to make forced stops on the basis of mere suspicion founded on profile characteristics. Overwhelmingly this policy has led to the random forced stop of young blacks. One study showed that 76 percent of all arrests for drugs and weapon violations made by random stops on the New Jersey Turnpike were black, far higher than state averages for those crimes or of use of the road by blacks. The profile approach to random forced stops helps to explain how in New York state more than 90 percent of new prison commitments for drug offenses were blacks and Latinos, even though only 13 percent of the nation's drug users are black. Race-based suspicion goes far to explaining why the 12 percent of the nation who are black serve 75 percent of the prison time for drug prohibition.[27]

Characteristics that DEA agents have offered as warranting forced stops include arriving from a "source city," defined as any major airport late at night or early in the morning, being one of the first or last to deplane, using a one-way or round-trip ticket, carrying new luggage or a gym bag, traveling alone or with a companion, acting nervously, dressing in black corduroys, a white shirt and loafers, wearing a brown leather aviator jacket or walking rapidly through the airport. Given these vague and general characteristics, it is not surprising how many wrongful forced stops are made. In a study at the Buffalo airport, only 10 of 600 people stopped were found to carry drugs. Drug war tactics work because they declare everyone a suspect, then sort out the public without regard for the consequence in civil liberties. Most people falsely detained never employ legal remedy, while the courts are deaf to the Constitutional arguments raised by those who were breaking the prohibitions.

Even in those rare instances in which the Constitutional mandate for a judicial warrant is upheld, the Court has weakened the importance of the Amendment. In *United States v. Leon* the Court upheld the use of a warrant issued upon illegal grounds deemed to be a genuine error.[28] Justice Brennan wrote regarding the relaxation of standards regarding warrants that "I have witnessed the Court's gradual but determined strangulation of the rule. It now appears that the Court's victory over the Fourth Amendment is complete."

In 1985 the Supreme Court accepted that a female international traveler could be held on profile suspicion and forced to defecate in a wastebasket. After 24 hours of incarceration she was still not allowed to call her lawyer. She was taken to a hospital for a forced rectal examination. The appeals court had overturned her conviction on Fourth Amendment grounds sighting the fundamental lack of humanity in such police practice. The Supreme Court ruled that this was a justifiable sacrifice of liberty interests.

The Court again diminished the Fourth Amendment in *Ohio v. Robinette*.[29] In that case a police officer stopped a car for speeding and then searched the car with the driver's consent but without informing the driver that he could decline. The search revealed a small amount of marijuana and one pill that turned out to be methamphetamine. The state court suppressed the drugs, finding that the warrantless search was coerced. The Supreme Court reversed the decision. Though they insisted the "Fourth Amendment test for a valid consent to search is that the consent be voluntary," in their view "voluntary" does not mean that the person knew he had a right to decline.

America's culture war has spread to an assault on the right to be represented by counsel. Murderers and rapists can employ counsel of their own selection. Under the Comprehensive Forfeiture Act, drug defendants are stripped of their assets and their lawyers are made defendants for acceptance of fees paid for representation. Defense lawyers must bargain with prosecution to keep their fees. The bargaining chip is terms for admission of guilt by the client. The very basis of advocacy is thus undermined. Attorney General Edwin Meese asserted that the value of the defense attorney as working against the prosecution but for a balanced contest of justice must be sacrificed in the drug context. Meese told a lawyer's conference that "there are no bystanders, not even the lawyers."[30] The *National Law Journal* reported "Government investigation of lawyers—including such tactics as informants, wiretaps, subpoenas and office searches—have risen so dramatically in the last 4 years that they are almost common."[31] Because of this assault on the defense bar there has emerged an exodus from the field, leaving those accused of such crimes to overworked government-employed public defenders whose basic job is to obtain an admission of guilt without the expense and risk of judicial process.

In *Caplin and Drysdale, Chartered v. United States*, Justice White endorsed "stripping criminals . . . of their undeserved economic power because this is to undermine the drug defendant's ability to command high priced talent."[32] The Court thus has accepted the mission of legitimating the government's purposeful undermining of the Constitutional promise of full right to defense council. Impoverished defendants take the public defender's offered deal.

The most fundamental notions of due process and fundamental fair play have been repeatedly sacrificed. In *United States v. Monsanto* the Court upheld the forfeiture of assets of persons not yet convicted of criminal action in disregard of the traditional presumption of innocence.[33] The government is able to accomplish through civil forfeiture punishment that might fail if they were forced to lead with criminal prosecution.

In *United States v. Usery*[34] the Supreme Court ruled that stripping a family of their home in a civil proceeding following conviction for growing personal use of marijuana is not "punishment" within the meaning of the Constitution and so does not violate the double jeopardy clause. The house was not bought with proceeds of drug sales, nor was the house bought to be a marijuana farm. There was no evidence of any sale of the crop at all. The family home was taken by summary process with no additional judicial hearing. The appeals court invoked double jeopardy to block this process but was overruled by the punishment-enthusiastic Supreme Court.

The Supreme Court again advanced the agenda of unrestrained punishment for cultural crimes in *Bennis v. Michigan*. In that case a man drove the family car while engaging in an act of prostitution. The state took the car, thus stripping the wife of her half of the common property and of her basic means of transportation. In dissent the moderate Justice Stevens asked, would a hotel thus be forfeit if an act of prostitution was discovered to have transpired there. He further probes, "For centuries prostitutes have been plying their trade on other people's property. . . . A profession of this vintage has provided government with countless opportunities to use novel weapons to curtail its abuse. As far as I am aware, however, it is not until 1988 that any state decided to experiment with the punishment of innocent third parties by confiscating property. . . ."[35] It is the theme of the next two chapters of this book to attempt to explain why the modern era has seen greater use of government to punish cultural behavior and greater sacrafice of the Constitutional heritage than ever before in American history.

The Court again sacrificed fundamental fairness to advance the cause of cultural punishment in *Neal v. United States*. In that case the defendant was sentenced to 10 years for possession of 4.58 grams of lysergic acid diethylamide (LSD). He was sentenced under statutes that required 10 years as the minimum sentence for 10 grams of the drug. The authorities failed to subtract the weight of the carrying medium paper from the weight of the actual drug and so determined that he possessed over 109 grams. The United States Sentencing Commission ruled that he should only be punished for the drug, not the packaging weight. Writing for the Court, Justice Kennedy submitted, "True, there may be little logic to defend the statute's treatment of L.S.D.; it results in significant disparity of punishment meted out. . . . Even so, Congress, not this Court has the responsibility for revising the statute."[36] In abrogation of the idea of an independent judiciary upholding fundamental fairness and promised restraint in the deployment of government's punishing authority, the Supreme Court overruled the Commission's interpretation of the statutes to achieve an interpretation that is less rational and more draconian.

Similar commitment to punitive abundance rather than fundamental fairness is expressed in *Carlisle v. United States*[37] After a trial for a federal marijuana violation, the defendant filed a motion that the judge review the merits of the prosecution's case to determine if it had produced sufficient evidence to achieve a verdict of guilty. Though the motion came 1 day after the 7-day limit, the trial court granted the motion and declared, "I believe that refusal to hear this motion would result in grave injustice." Failure of the defense lawyer to file in a timely manner to the district court could not outweigh in the balance of justice that the prosecution simply had not proven its case. The Supreme Court overturned the trial court and reinstated the punishment. The Supreme Court instructed that the trial court had no right to rely on inherent authority or due process powers to achieve substantive justice. In dissent Justice Stevens writes, "As long as a federal court retains jurisdiction over a criminal case, it has the authority to insure that no conviction is entered unless the prosecuter has proved the defendant's guilt. The exercise of the court's inherent power to set aside a jury verdict unsupported by evidence is not contingent on the filing of a timely motion by the defendant."[38]

As oversight of the plea-bargaining process, the Court has

ensured that deals work against the interest of the accused regardless of fairness and rights. In *Melendez v. United States*[39] the defendant pleaded guilty and cooperated with prosecuters in return for an agreed sentence below the statutory minimum of 10 years for conspiracy to buy 5 kilograms of cocaine. The Supreme Court imposed the 10-year sentence based on the guilty plea, thus the defendant was induced to give up his right to a trial and received no benefit from his cooperation. In *Libretti v. United States*[40] the defendant had similar cause to believe that by Supreme Court action, the entirety of the process operated to preclude fundamental fairness. In that case the defendant accepted a plea bargain, and then subsequently the government initiated forfeiture on additional assets. The Supreme Court ruled that the govenment is not required to inform the defendant that the plea bargain opens the door for subsequent forfeiture without jury deliberation or due process rights. Thus he was unable to argue the factual claim that these assets were outside the statutory bounds of forfeiture. In dissent Justice Stevens wrote, "the law defines the outer boundaries of a permissable forfeiture."

Perhaps the most sweeping example that the Supreme Court sees itself in the role of facilitating mass punishment rather than upholding Constitutional rights or providing a fair forum for dispute is provided in a 1997 summary decision. This decision upheld a sentencing practice of the judge increasing the length of incarceration augmented by charges dismissed by a jury as though the charges had been proven. By a 7-to-2 vote, the Court agreed that federal judges may use these rejected charges to impose incarceration terms that exceed the maximum otherwise allowed by statute.

In one such case a federal judge added to the defendant's conviction for one ounce of cocaine the penalty for a second charge of participation in the sale of 5 ounces for which he was declared not guilty. Justice Stevens labeled the Supreme Court's endorsement of this shabby process "perverse" and "repugnant" and antithetical to "the traditional requirement that criminal charges must be sustained by proof beyond a reasonable doubt."[41] Justice Stevens went on to point out that there is no statutory basis for this practice. The federal guidelines call for adjustment to sentencing based on prior convictions, not on unproven charges.

The most troubling aspect of this memorandum decision is that neither the dissenting justice nor the defendant and his attorneys were permitted to participate in it. The Court issued its ruling based only on the initial brief filed by the Justice Department. Hence there were no alternative briefs read or oral arguments considered. Facilitation of punitive abundance is the only value thus served.

The Warren Court focused its creativity and authority to eliminate legally enforced racial division and to move the nation toward racial justice through constitutional law. The Rehnquist Court has worked to the opposite ends by using the authority of the War on Drugs to inflict a new chapter of racial oppression. In *United States v. Armstrong* the Court legitimated the federal practice of prosecuting black drug users and sellers at far harsher rates with longer resulting sentences than white drug users and sellers.[42] The Court further shielded the prosecution from the need to defend against the statistically true claim of harsh preferential treatment for punishment of blacks by ruling that only if a bias is shown for punishing this individual minority defendant is there basis for further review. This despite a showing by the defendants that every person prosecuted by the federal office in 1991 was black. Whites were alternatively left to far more lenient state jurisdiction.

Justice Stevens in his dissenting opinion clarified the heart of the matter. Federal law under the 1986 Anti-Drug Abuse Act calls for a 100 times greater punishment for crack cocaine than for pure cocaine. The racist and classist nature of federal prosecution is thus not the result of discrimination on the part of the federal prosecutor. Racist and classist penalties are written right into the federal laws and are the deliberative product of the political system. The Court in this case is merely allowing a punishment-hungry body politic to have its way.

In sum, the Supreme Court and the Constitution are no longer significant factors in deterring the translation of cultural definitions of sin into criminal prosecution. Nor are they significant in limiting the means used by the police in the waging of this culture war. In fact the Court has taken on a mission of advancing the War on Drugs and other cultural prosecutions in disregard of their mandate to uphold the text of the Constitution. In this behavior they are very much acting as people of this age of popular punitive abundance rather than as ageless preserves of tradition and heritage. The American people are not protected from abuse of the criminal justice system by the Constitution or the Supreme Court. Politics is rather the source of criminal law. The heart of criminal justice policy lies in discovering the sociology of our age that fosters the punishment movement and the translation of that sociology into politics and law.

NOTES

1. Joseph Gusfield, *Symbolic Crusade: Status, Politics and the American Temperance Movement* (Urbana, University of Illinois Press, 1963).
2. 277 U.S. 438 (1928).
3. Ibid.
4. Ibid.
5. 354 U.S. 298 (1957).
6. 381 U.S. 479 (1965).
7. 410 U.S. 113 (1973).
8. 394 U.S. 557 (1969).
9. 367 U.S. 643 (1961).
10. Ibid.
11. 389 U.S. 347 (1967).
12. "Chief Justice Makes Plea for More Federal Judgeships to Help in the Fight Against Drugs," *New York Times*, Jan. 1, 1990.
13. John Decker, *Revolution to the Right* (New York, Garland, 1992).
14. Ibid.
15. A.B.C. News Poll, *Washington Post*, Sept. 8, 1989.
16. 504 U.S. 655 (1992).
17. Ibid.
18. 501 U.S. 429 (1991).
19. Ibid.
20. *Skinner v. Railway Labor Executives' Association*, 489 U.S. 602 (1989).
21. *Richards v. Wisconsin*, No. 96–5955 (1997).

22. 466 U.S. 170 (1984).
23. *California v. Aceredo*, 500 U.S. 565 (1991).
24. 469 U.S. 325 (1985).
25. 499 U.S. 621 (1991).
26. 113 Sup. Ct. 2130 (1993).
27. *Drug Policy Newsletter*, Number 28, Winter 1996.
28. 468 U.S. 897 (1984).
29. U.S. Sup. Ct. 95–891 (1997).
30. Dan Baum, *Smoke and Mirrors: The War on Drugs and the Politics of Failure* (Boston, Little Brown, 1996).
31. *National Law Journal* 7 (27), March 18, 1985.
32. 491 U.S. 617 (1989).
33. 491 U.S. 600 (1989).
34. 116 Sup. Ct. 2135 (1996).
35. 116 Sup. Ct. 994 (1996).
36. 116 Sup. Ct. 763 (1996).
37. 116 Sup. Ct. 1460 (1996).
38. "Chief Justice Makes Plea for More Federal Judgeships to Help in the Fight Against Drugs," *New York Times*, January 1, 1990.
39. 116 Sup. Ct. 2057 (1996).
40. 116 Sup. Ct. 356 (1995).
41. Order No. 97–5122, October 6, 1997.
42. 116 Sup. Ct. 1480 (1996).

4

The Symbolic Importance of Drugs

In the pursuit of the War on Drugs, society has sacrificed its fundamental covenant on liberty as well as its financial well-being, integrity of its police and benevolent orientation of its public sector. The fundamental relationships of many citizens to government has changed from progressive paternalism to aggressive authoritarianism.

What motivation could have driven such sweeping collapse of the prior liberal commitments? The question answers itself; a powerful will to undermine liberalism is the root cause and the use of the War on Drugs. Drug pleasures became a powerful metaphor for moral decay and so assault on drug use emerged as a prime weapon for the restoration of traditional unliberal culture. Drugs as a metaphor for undesired culture and assault on drug users as a weapon in the restoration of conservative rule is the big story of the anti-drug hysteria. The War on Drugs fervor became a battering ram to demolish the disliked programs and policies of the past liberal order. This is paralleled and reinforced by the use of drug policy in race and class control. Chapter Five will switch to the pieces of the smaller related stories of how drug hate served the interests of particular politicians, government agencies, media, promoters of fundamentalist religion, racial conflict and other profiteers off the war. This chapter places the use of drug hate in the big picture of ideological conflict and generational tension.

The principle objection to viewing the War on Drugs as an essential piece of grand ideological conflict is to argue that drugs are sufficiently inherently unhealthy that no additional motivation is needed to justify mass criminalization. A quick review of basic facts preclude granting even minimal credence to the claim that the drug war is really about promotion of public health. During the period of this punitive public policy the nation in fact considered and rejected the idea of extending health benefits to working class and poor persons. Cost of providing public health was of course a prime factor in the debate. The cost of mass incarceration under the domestic war was never considered a transferable portion of the public health budget. The War on Drugs throughout the debate was regarded as a separate untouchable punitive agenda.

Ninety-five percent of the nation's illegal drug users smoke marijuana exclusively. The term "gateway drug" sometimes used to describe it, is false; only a small percentage of its users ever move into hard drugs. Over the last decades numerous objective studies were commissioned on the health implications of smoking marijuana. All have concluded that criminalization of the user is a far greater health hazard than any inherent property of the drug itself. The Kaiser Foundation, after reviewing all studies of marijuana, concluded that there is no evidence of the use of marijuana as cause of any life-threatening health condition.

During the modern offensive against marijuana, the inhaling of legal toxic chemicals has replaced pot as the high of choice in many juvenile circles. Though these inhalants carry harsh medical implications, they do not have the cultural baggage of pot and so are preferred by implication of policy. Marijuana has never been listed as a cause of anyone's death, and there is no such thing in practice as an overdose quantity.

Scholarly European reports concerning the social consequences of use of this drug might begin with the British-sponsored *Indian Hemp Drug Commission of 1893–1894*. This report concluded that "viewing the subject generally, it must be added that the moderate use of these drugs is the rule, and that the excessive use is comparatively exceptional. The moderate use produces practically no ill effects."

The first scientifically based American study is the *Panama Canal Zone Military Investigations, 1916–1929*. This report determined that "there is no evidence that Marihuana as grown and used is a habit forming drug." They recommended that "no step be taken by the Canal Zone authorities to prevent the sale or use of Marihuana."

An early extensive study of drug use in the urban environment is the Mayor's Committee on Marijuana, otherwise known as the *La Guardia Report*. This 1944 study determined that "the publicity concerning the catastrophic effects of marihuana smoking in New York is unfounded." This report agreed with prior studies that showed that smoking marijuana is nonaddictive and does not lead to undesired behaviors.

The most extensive government-sponsored study to date is the 1973 report published by the President Nixon–appointed Commission on Marihuana and Drug Abuse. Finding no significant health consequence, the Commission's report recommended the decriminalization of small sales of marijuana and legalization of personal use. After selecting this panel, President Nixon repudiated its results. The findings did not fit into his political strategy of deploying police authority against cultural deviance to create a majority coalition based on enforced social traditionalism.

The most scholarly report to date was produced by the prestigious National Research Council of the National Academy of Sciences in 1982. They recommended total withdrawal of the federal government from marijuana policy. They concluded that decriminalization where it has been practiced has not increased use and that the current policy of arresting hordes of users each year is a national tragedy. Most recently the *New England Journal of Medicine* (Jan. 30, 1997) concluded the continued criminalization of the medical use of marijuana was unconscionable given the broad use of the drug by oncologists and for treatment of AIDS nausea. In 1997 a commission of the National Institutes of Health called for the drug to be regarded as a schedule II medicine to be regulated by the Food and Drug Administration.

The bottom line for the nation's dominant illegal drug is that there are zero fatalities in medical history for marijuana use. This compares to nearly a half million deaths each year from tobacco and tens of thousands of deaths each year from alcohol, the nation's number one and number two drugs in health consequence. Clearly something other than concern for public health is driving drug policy. The health risk of marijuana is predominantly that almost half a million Americans each year are drawn into the criminal justice system through the prohibition of this drug.

Even if the standard for health consequence is changed from hard medical evidence of physical harm to sociological and psychological damage the evidence is not there to justify criminalization. At the University of California at Berkeley in a long-term study two psychologists followed 100 children from the ages of 5 to 18 to determine the effects of moderate use of drugs, mostly marijuana, as compared to total abstinence and heavy use of drugs.[1] This study, published in *American Psychologist*, determined that problem drug use was predicted by poor parenting in the earliest phases of childhood. Hence, problem drug use is a symptom of personal maladjustment not treatable with criminal prosecution. Total drug abstinence occurred in children who were relatively anxious, emotionally constricted, and lacking in social skills. Moderate recreational drug use was exhibited among the best adjusted of the children and was positively correlated to subsequent academic performance and admission to elite colleges.

In the marijuana context, the scientific material has mounted regarding therapeutic uses. Medical marijuana has received strong anecdotal recommendations from persons suffering nausea due to chemotherapy, persons suffering the wasting effect of AIDS, glaucoma patients and migraine headache sufferers. In 1988 persons benefiting from the medical use of marijuana assembled their case before an administrative law judge of the Drug Enforcement Agency. After reviewing the evidence of real medical benefit to marijuana, Judge Francis Young wrote, "it is clear beyond any question that many people find marijuana to have accepted medical use in treatment."[2] Further he found "marijuana in its natural form is one of the safest therapeutically active substances known to man." His finding included comparison to the relatively dangerous drug of common aspirin. The major impediment to more data emerging on the therapeutic effects of marijuana is the DEA's designation of the drug as schedule I, not suited for study or use under any condition. Accordingly when medical groups attempted to conduct controlled studies of use of the drug they were informed that such science would be subject to criminal prosecution. This designation is a portion of the growing mass of evidence that drug policy is fueled by ideological allegiance rather than health policy or public safety.

Other evidence that ideology rather than public health fuels the drug war is found in the criminalization of intravenous needles. Over half of all AIDS cases contracted in the 1990s were as a result of needle sharing among intravenous drug users. This statistic understates the anti-health effect of the War on Drugs. In the new era of proteas inhibitor drugs, some AIDS patients can recover. However, AIDS patients who contracted the virus through shared needles are likely to have contracted hepatitis C, and so not be able to tolerate the new drugs. A public health orientation should demand provision of clean needles to fight this modern plague. This is the routine practice across Europe. That the War on Drugs has fought against clean needles is more evidence that public health concern does not drive this policy agenda. Lacking the American interest in fighting a domestic culture war, the British have placed heroin under the control of the medical profession to be administered to addicts.

If more evidence is needed that cultural conflict rather than concern for public health is at the heart of this domestic war, it is found in the relative treatment of traditional drugs as opposed to counter-culture and ethnic drugs. No drug causes more harm in the United States than tobacco. Nicotine as a substance is highly addictive, far more addictive than cocaine or alcohol and rivals heroin, according to the Surgeon General, in the cravings that its withdrawal produces. It causes over 400,000 deaths annually, hundreds of times more than any other drug, while marijuana, the focal drug of the drug war is not attributed with any deaths. There is more public health reason to declare war on tobacco than on any other drug. What is lacking for such engagement is cultural hate of tobacco users and, at least until recently, the limited potential for political profit from exploitation of the issue. Revelation that the tobacco industry spiked their product so as to enhance their addictive hold on users created an awareness by the Clinton administration that this issue was ripe for greater political gain. The relative punishment of crack, often a drug of blacks, compared to real cocaine, a majority white drug, furthers understanding of the cultural foundation of the war.

Alcohol is the nation's second greatest drug problem. Like tobacco, it has more objective basis for criminalization than most illegal drugs. Health consequences of alcohol include addiction, depression, liver damage, brain damage and, for 100,000 consumers each year, death. Social ramifications include increased hostility and impaired reasoning and response time most significantly affecting driving ability. Like tobacco, its place among white average populations preclude criminal sanction. When the cultural equation in the beginning of the century stood with Irish, Italian and German immigrants as the most popularly disliked groups, criminalization of their drug of choice led to Prohibition and its drug war–like policy failures and political uses.

If public health were a genuine priority for American politics, the whole funding priority for drug punishment would be irrational. Each year 50,000 persons are damaged from lead poisoning as opposed to fewer than 4,000 fatal overdoses for all illegal drugs. At far less expense and with much greater public health return than the criminalization of forbidden drug pleasures society could scrape and paint old homes, replace old water pipes that contaminate water delivery and inoculate children to a range of disease. Finally, of course, however bad some illegal drugs may be for some people, prison is almost certainly worse. Public health is provided by doing positive things in society. The will for massive punishment held by some of the American people is motivated by other interests.

Having rejected the public health justification for this domestic war, nonbenevolent explanations must be considered, among which is the view that the criminalization of drugs is a means toward public safety. While in some instances this may in fact be the intent, it clearly is not the effect. Disruption of the drug trade leads to market segment rivalry. Given the inability to settle conflict in court or through advertizing or other normal means of business engagement, this conflict typically becomes violent. When under the Bush administration the drug market in the nation's capital became the target of mass incarceration, the murder rate rose sharply as old market groups were broken up and new ones jostled for the niche.

Even the nation's most violence-instilling drug, alcohol, was subject to this trend. Intoxicated people are given to boisterous, reckless and aggressive behavior. But the criminalization of alcohol sales did not reduce this effect. Instead the distribution market under the conditions of prohibition became gun laden and violent. The gangs of the Prohibition era and their violence is an epic story of the nation's history. Once Franklin Roosevelt lifted Prohibition, liquor companies shifted their form of competition from strong-arm tactics to more typical deployment of accountants and lawyers. Even the most passive drug, marijuana, becomes a source of violence when prohibition causes the growers and distributors to become criminal. Thus as Campaign Against Marijuana Production (CAMP)–targeted growers in Humboldt County, flower-children growers were replaced over time with armed, production aggressive–minded entrepreneurs.

American and British studies find that heroin users left to themselves are less violent than the average of society at large. This result led the British to take the problem of heroin away from law enforcement and place it under a medical approach. Britain accordingly enjoys a far lower rate of violence in its heroin market. Significantly, it also enjoys a lower rate of heroin use. By remaining free of the effects of criminalization and incarceration, British users are able to maintain productive lives as users and eventually voluntarily end their addiction. Study in the United States shows that heroin users left to themselves do not gravitate toward violence.[3] When drug markets stabilize they achieve a passivity. Of all violence related to drug use, 98 percent is drug merchants defending their market niche, less than 2 percent is users raising funds for purchase. The targeting of drug markets by police busts is a source of increased violence rather than public safety. A significant factor in the decline of violence in the 1990s is maturation and stabilization of the drug markets. In addition as American heroin users suffer incarceration and criminal records, their odds of turning their lives about diminish.

Given the absence of both public health and public safety benefits to drug criminalization it becomes necessary to look deeper into social forces to find justification for the centrality American politics and culture places on fighting its war with users of forbidden drugs. Given the intensity and long duration of this self-imposed and popular domestic war and the absence of tangible benefits from its expense and the manifest harm it has wrought, the search for motivation is not a small or unimportant task. Finding the roots of the drug war is an exploration into the soul of American civilization. It is a search that involves elements of intergenerational conflict, conflict between Traditionalists and persons with a will to social change, ethnic and racial conflict, conflict between believers in the liberal promises of individual liberty and pursuit of happiness and their critics, conflict over the emergence of the welfare state and, at the most profound level, conflict over alternative models of spirituality and divinity. In sum, to tell the story of the nation's obsession with illegal drugs is to touch on the whole contemporary story of civilization. The War on Drugs *is* ultimately a genuine domestic war. It can only be analyzed by considering the same passions and loyalties, hates and other motivations that are used in considering other eras in which the raw power of the state is turned on its own population.

A pivotal juncture in the exacerbation of drug hate is the rise of the Reagan Revolution and its surrounding sociology and politics. In a national poll conducted contemporaneously with the rise of this conservative coalition, the American people predicted with unusual accuracy that the coming decade would mark a decided increase in all aspects of government engagement in control of personal life.[4] Three out of 4 polled persons believed the "right to privacy" should be akin to the inalienable rights to life, liberty and the pursuit of happiness. Yet by a 51 percent to 38 percent majority the public believed that in 10 years "we will have lost our ability to keep important aspects of our lives from government." Overwhelming majorities of both the general public and a special poll of persons designated as leaders felt that law enforcement agencies should not be able to open mail, tap telephones, or look at bank records of persons suspected of criminal activity but not convicted of a crime without a court order.

Large majorities of the public believed that homosexual relations in private between consenting adults are areas of personal choice that should be left to the individual and not regulated or forbidden by law. Majorities felt similarly about an individual's decision to have an abortion or to smoke marijuana. The leadership poll showed concurrence with all these results, with the only exception registered by officials in the law enforcement agencies.

In the years after this poll the whole topic of personal privacy became an intense battle ground. Abortion and the surrounding matters of the sexual revolution, gay rights, multiculturalism and the counter-culture all were declared targets by the Reagan administration. There was an intense will in government and in much of society to undo the many changes that had occurred in the prior 3 decades of social change. Assault on drugs like assault on abortion rights, open sexuality and gay rights was a means for rejection of what had become defined as bad New Age culture.

Marijuana as a 1960s' symbol of peace, freedom and new culture, the coming out of gay identity and gay pride movements in the 1970s, abortion and the loosening of sexual rules from the late 1950s through the 1990s all are portions of a vast social and political change highly disapproved of by the conservative 1980s ruling coalition. The emphatic criminalization of marijuana in the 1980s and early 1990s was every bit as driven by symbolic meaning as the drug craze of the 1960s was driven by its own symbolism. As one counter-culture expression worded the matter, "the issue is not the issue." Marijuana was never the public health or safety concern the conservative forces contended nor the means to personal enlightenment the counterculture maintained. But both found in marijuana a symbolism, for the counter-culture of the narrowness and rules obsession of dominant society and for conservatives of the breakdown of moral order. Praise of marijuana, LSD., and later cocaine was as much a portion of the liberation zeitgeist of the 1960s and 1970s as drug hate was of the traditional values revolution in the 1980s and 1990s. Both were intricately linked to the larger cultural maps of these two eras. The decades of free love are followed by the decades of drug hate in a complex contemporary dialectic that has molded this age.

The liberation movements of the liberal decades were expressions of a view that the rules and conventions of the larger society prevented individuals from achieving their personal potential. Michel Foucault in studying the asylums and prisons of Europe concluded that the use of these institutions was not public health or safety, but rather social control.[5] People who cannot conform are segregated for the benefit of enforcing the orthodox order. Sigmund Freud in *Civilization and Its Discontents*[6] argues that there is an unending battle between those who like a world of rules and order against those who are drawn to creativity and disorder. The orthodox and the reformers are locked in dialectic confrontation with as much continuity as Marx's dialectical confrontation between workers and owners. The orthodox persecute the rebels to regain control from contaminating new expressions. Drug culture became the most disliked form of unorthodoxy and so the focal target for the defending guns of state authority. Criminal justice was unleashed to defend cultural order by massive prosecution of the discontent.

The conflict arises because the liberated person's individual identity is often not tolerable to the orthodox order. Foucault wanted to raise the tolerance of society and lower the individual's fear of indulging the inner longings. He counseled that you as an individual needed to learn how to "become yourself" in violation of the taboos and criminal justice system of the day. Forbidden drug and sexual experiences were a means to setting the repressed self free. Homosexuality, bi-sexuality, sadomasochism and LSD and other drugs were tools by which the individual confronted repressive orthodox order and found the will to become him- or herself.

Social movements across America acted out the search for new identity and the subsequent reform of social order to make room for previously intolerable self-expression. Events and social forces came together to form a deep belief among large segments of American society that something had gone very wrong in the construction of traditional social order. Only if individuals were freed to search for new ways could real social happiness and social evolution occur.

There is no conclusively correct explanation of why so many different groups decided in the same era that a social liberation was necessary and possible. One factor certainly was reaction to the brooding anger manifest in the McCarthy era and its search for deviance within the nation and conviction that all individuality is an expression of evil named communism but not distinguishable from many other things such as liberalism, tolerance, charity or individualism.[7] Accordingly a search throughout the government, media, education and unions was conducted to uproot all opposition to social orthodoxy in the name of patriotism.

In its zeal to weed out social deviance, the federal government created a personality assessment test to keep the federal bureaucracy morally conforming.[8] Questions asked included the following: "Were you a regular reader of the *New York Times*?"; "Do you and your wife regularly attend church service?"; "What do you think of female chastity?"; "Have you ever had Negroes in your home?"; and, "In your library at home, could you give me an idea of the books that you enjoy accumulating?" The implication is that intelligence, broad awareness and cultural diversity among public officials are a threat to the nation. From this piece of policy it is easy to extrapolate that the McCarthy era was a high point for rule lovers and orthodoxy protection, thus ripe for a rebellion by the "discontent" in the Freudian dialectic.

The Kennedy presidency forms a clear contrast to this demand for conformity. The simple fact of President Kennedy's victory over the McCarthy-era figure Richard Nixon signaled an important milestone in social movement away from the search for radicals. Further, Kennedy's victory marked a reduction in the level of endorsement of formal conservative religion by the government. In the primary election period there was objection to allowing for the first Catholic president. The fear raised in much of America was inherited from prejudice drawn out of European history. Would a Catholic be so faithful to the Vatican and the surrounding orthodoxy as to transform the many religious prohibitions into lawful force? In repeatedly rebutting that question, Kennedy vowed that the Church would have absolutely no claim on his political views. Kennedy made as vigorous a statement for the affirmation of the separation of religion and government as any since Thomas Jefferson. With this assertion of Enlightenment ideals, a questioning of much in the law was in order. Other than an endorsement of traditional religious values, why were birth control, sex out of wedlock, oral sex and homosexuality all criminal acts? When the President renounced allegiance to the church, a questioning of the rules became fashionable for others. In Kennedy's public message that "The torch of leadership has passed to a new generation," many who wished to question the old rules found further endorsement of the idea that they had presidential leadership in exploring the frontiers of a new social era. If a new generation has assumed leadership, must it endorse all the old rules of order?

Later politicians would learn that by emphasizing the sinful aspect of the human potential they could distract the public from the withdrawal of positive government. In this liberal era Kennedy practiced the reciprocal wisdom that by emphasizing the positive of human potential it was possible to call government away from the angry McCarthy-era negative agenda and to progressive initiatives. Arthur Schlesinger summarized, "I think that he sensed there were great reserves of idealism in the American people, pent up after eight years."[9] By focusing on the positive potential in people, Kennedy drew the nation to agendas like the elimination of poverty and exploration of space and so away from the search for nonconformity. Kennedy's gradual adoption of the civil rights agenda further bolstered this positive definition of the use of government. Emphasis on government promotion of the arts and culture further redirected the nation's attention away from internal deviance and threats to tradition.

One quote hauntingly summarizes the nation's involvement with Kennedy. "Those who would make peaceful change impossible make violent revolution inevitable."[10] The assassination of President Kennedy may well be hypothesized as a link in the chain of events that changed the relationship of the people to government. This act of violence legitimated a wave of rule breaking in which people disregarded law and tradition and made forbidden decisions in their own lives. With a ferocity that rivaled the opposite sentiment during the McCarthy era, a segment of American society in the following years expressed their mistrust of the establishment and began to insist that the government leave the individual alone. In this "Age of Aquarius," drug taking was one of several personal acts of rebellion.[11] When the ages changed again in the "Reagan Revolution," such rebellions would become harshly criminalized in a crusade to quash the culture of self-liberation and restore orthodox traditional culture.

Persistant revelations of the immorality and criminality of the government's behavior in other sectors continued the sense that the power of law had gone wrong. The FBI under J. Edgar Hoover was exposed as using federal power to undermine Martin Luther King, Jr. and promote racism, while tolerating and denying the existence of real organized crime. Further, the Johnson and, to a greater degree, Nixon presidencies were operated with contempt to democracy and political law. All of this furthered the social sense that the rules and rulers were wrong and that the individual must make decisions without regard to restrictions.

The counter-culture fed off this condemnation of the status quo. Awareness of the deep wrongness in adult culture gave the baby-boomers a sense that rule breaking was a moral imperative. Drug taboos became a favorite means of personal rebellion.

Drugs, of course, go back well into prehistory. From antiquity, Native Americans have used peyote in religious ceremonies, Mexicans used marijuana for centuries and native South Americans traditionally used the base plant of cocaine.[12] Europeans traditionally used alcohol and founded the Virginia colony for tobacco production as they developed a taste for it. Other ethnic groups brought other drugs into the American mix, such as Chinese use of opium. So drug use as an act itself by Americans in the 1960s and 1970s is only a normal state of human tastes. What is different is the political and social meaning that rebellious Americans attached to their consumption.

Drug consumption became an aspect of a rising counter-culture that blossomed in the notions of immorality held by the dominant culture and was fed from the energy of the emerging baby boom. One month after the Kennedy slaying, the Beatles gave their famed American television debut. The centrality in the emerging youth culture of the Beatles and other artists who joined in the celebration of non-conformity as a freedom life-style, extended the importance of psychedelic art as a spiritual focus of life. John Lennon would set the pattern for the heart of the drug war. As a media star he used his celebrity to attack the Vietnam War, capitalism and the conformist life-style. When the government moved against him, it was his conviction for marijuana that became the tool for the ideologically desired deportation proceedings. The criminalization of the drug use of undesirables allowed government the tool to deploy larger punitive policies against the counter-culture and defend the orthodox order. Lennon could only sing out about "imagin(ing) there's no state or religion."

The power of art and drugs as liberationist forces in the 1960s flows from the prior avant-garde cultural forces of the Beatniks and associated voices. In folk music and written verse, an art theme had developed that emphasized criticism of conformity and reveled in self-exploration and self-growth. Leading the list of literary works with this message are *The Catcher in the Rye* by J. D. Salinger, *Brave New World* by Aldous Huxley, *On the Road* by Jack Kerouac and the poetry of Allen Ginsberg. All of these authors mixed drug use and writing to find expression in which they confronted the larger society.

Even Hollywood turned its attention to the Foucault-like theme of personal liberation through rule breaking. This theme took early form with works such as *The Wild Ones* and *Rebel Without a Cause*. Later *The Graduate, Easy Rider* and *Five Easy Pieces* extended the idea that the larger society with its many rules was hypocritical and wrong. The individual can only find enlightened growth through looking inward and finding his or her own path. For many this path included forbidden art, sex and drugs.

The Kinsey Report, *Sexual Behavior in the Human Male*,[13] stands as an enduring statement of how false the conservative model of sexuality had become. Based on over 10,000 interviews, the study revealed that 80 percent of males, according to the rules of their states, were sexual criminals. Most states at the time had rules against oral sex, fornication, adultery, homosexuality, and prostitution. The Kinsey Report was the first source to document how broadly human these criminalized sins were. Other revelations included that women often liked and sought sex, a distinctly unacceptable conclusion to 1950s morality. Vehement denunciation of the study by conservative religious institutions as leading to immorality only served to heighten the awareness that dominant society had fallen so deeply under the control of moralists that it no longer could deal in reality. This realization fueled the sexual revolution, as first youths and then others began to openly disregard the old sexual laws and taboos.

A sexual revolution followed that changed the criminal code from a mass enforcer of conservative religious ideas of propriety. Across the nation adultery was struck from the criminal code. So too fornication, sex between unmarried people, commonly exited the criminal code. So too oral sex and other forms of the former crime of sodomy. Homosexuality, once a criminal act in every state, was accepted in half the states. The Kinsey Report showed that the majority of adults were criminals under the old criminal code. The laws changed, legally absolving most of them.

This realization that the rules of society enforced a code of morality that was oppressive and widely violated spread into realms outside sex. On college and university campuses across the nation, the old rules of curfews and mandatory housemothers for girls and mandatory military training and discipline for boys broke down. In curriculum the old canon of Latin and classics gave way to the rise of electives and diverse, multicultural course offerings. At the University of California at Berkeley, then at other campuses, students fought for and sometimes received the right to practice a broader sphere of speech on campus.

The oppressive demands for social conformity in the work place furthered the claim that the fundamental rules need to be broken as a means to freeing the individual and subsequently freeing society. Here sociological works, such as *The Lonely Crowd* by David Riesman, *The Organization Man* by William Whyte and *White Collar: The American Middle Class* by C. Wright Mills presented the view that life even for the fortunate and successful under the established order was also dull and sterile. All of these works and more shared the view that life in corporate, bureaucratic, suburban America stressed conformity to the point of losing the potential joy of life.

The baby-boom generation felt it deserved more. It believed in the freedom promised in the Constitution and by stories of the wild west and in animated adventure. Drugs came to play a significant role in the experience of forbidden freedom and the breaking of rules as the way to create a new self and a new society.

Perhaps the most passionate advocate of the need and right of the individual to achieve self-recreation through psychedelic experience is the author of *One Flew Over the Cuckoo's Nest*, Ken Kesey. He was perfectly set to be the storyteller of the emerging freedom-demanding youth movement. From his writer's retreat in the coastal mountains of California, he gathered a band of "merry pranksters" who joined him in roaming the nation like a Robin Hood troop committing "acid-tests." The test in the end was to drop acid, experience uncontrolled weirdness, think about it and be changed by the experience. Society played its role in this story by criminalizing him for the possession of marijuana, demonstrating the message that to be free in conformist America is to attract the sanction of a controlling conservative order.

That message is the theme of his first novel. The hero in *One Flew Over the Cuckoo's Nest* dares to challenge the oppressive order of the hospital administration. Although he is lobotomized in retribution by the orthodox hospital authorities, he changes the local culture and so liberates the other captive patients. The man of nature, an Indian chief, finds the will to return to the woods and be strong. A perfect myth for post-McCarthy-era America grappling with oppressive puritanic rules.

Ken Kesey, like Aldous Huxley before him and Michel Foucault, recognized drug experience as the taboo which the crossing of changes the identity of the seeker. For Aldous Huxley, author of *A Brave New World* and *Island*, modern technology had an unintended consequence of driving primitive emotion out of the increasingly pampered users. Psychedelics, a term of his creation, might jar the well-prepared searcher out of the confines of sterile existence and linear thought. So at Oxford and Cambridge Universities where he served on the faculties, he coached doctoral students through LSD use as a rite of passage.

Kesey, of course, took a much more mass-marketing approach. Both agreed in essence with Foucault that the great mission was to "become yourself." Society with its taboos and conventions played the role of defense against the seeker who might by sufficient exploration achieve knowledge of a forbidden but enlightened unique self.

Psychological study of LSD users does not validate the claim Kesey and the hippies that followed made of a comprehensive personality reordering. Only one aspect of personality and aptitude seems to shift. After intoxication users changed their priority in life goals away from money and materialism and toward the value of a contemplative life. Life experience rather than material outcome became the goal, process over results as the priority.[14]

Haight Ashbury became a prototypical American experience in pagan excess that was Aquarian liberation for some and the place of darkness for many more. This embrace of a living uncontrolled gathering composed of post "acid test" mass drug orgies, rock music jams and love-fests to the hippies was an experience of heaven on earth that spread to other cities across the nation. It simultaneously formed a battle cry to the orthodox that heavy criminalization was needed to restore order and decency. Governor Reagan was the man of the times who rose to the challenge of criminalizing the new culture wholesale to preserve moral tradition. In doing so he was thrust into the vanguard of America's emerging culture war and became a champion to the forces of traditional moral order. The hippies challenged the dominant culture through exotic and esoteric spiritual belief, pagan ecstatic festivals, as well as altered reasoning that placed ecstasy in substitute for stability as the prime value. Through new forms of art, drama, music and community they defied the old order. Thousands of youths flocked to the Haight Ashbury to join in this awakening. Tens of thousands more wove elements of this emerging counter-culture into their own lives and communities. They would soon learn just how hard society can push back when a successful counter-culture begins to challenge the orthodox order.

In the mass culture marijuana rather than LSD became the central drug of rebellion, self-liberation and discovery. There is no demonstrated long-term physiological impact from the use of marijuana. However, the simple act of breaking the law, enjoying the forbidden pleasure, then realizing that all government publications on the topic are false and all government laws morally wrong and socially repressive, may in its own way be radicalizing. That is the thesis of *The Greening of America* by Charles Reich. He wrote:

> Suppose that a straight college athlete, never interested in politics, tries marijuana. It will inevitably lead him to political and ideological concerns. Finding that the drug is comparatively harmless but nevertheless illegal, his credulity about laws will be strained. Realizing that far more harmful substances are legal, such as tobacco, alcohol, and various nonprescription drugs, he will begin to see that banning marijuana presents an ideological rather than a scientific question. Seeing that alcohol and tobacco yield huge profits to industry and are pressed on people by high-pressure advertising that insist they are "good" for you, he may draw some general conclusions about profits, morality and power in the corporate state.[15]

Reich's thesis while partially correct also proved to have tragic errors. The correct portion was the insight that drugs joined with sex and nonconformist cultural expressions, including music, visual arts and drama, to articulate a broad-based liberation of belief and actions. This coalition of social forces shared, as Foucault summarized, "a will not to be governed," and would in time birth an active gay rights movement that would strive for the next generation to achieve full equal acceptance for homosexuals. These cultural forces were also deeply entwined with a peace movement that successfully challenged the Vietnam War and created a reluctance against military engagement that lasted for decades. This counter-culture also grappled with environmental degradation in a manner not otherwise found in American politics. Protest against the prevailing political order manifested in the 1968 Democratic Party Convention held in Chicago that became a rallying point for a democratization of the primary process for presidential candidate selection.

At its most basic level people who broke the rules, who found the rules and rulers wrong, would then find themselves criminalized in turn. They pushed an array of issues for a shift of power away from established forces and back to the people, particularly to the individual. This democratization of authority and promotion of anarchy was expected to yield a greater tolerance for diversity which would cease the prosecution of nonconformity. Many groups joined in the general liberation. They included Native Americans, blacks, women and people striving for less institutional and more primitive spiritual expression—often summed up as New Age. Each of the many groups demanded a particular form of liberation: the sum total yielded an enormous demand for the loosening of the rules.

Reich was incorrect in two regards. The lesser error was in the degree to which participants of the social revolution would transfer their personal non-conformity into a call to political action. Believing the rhetoric of the social revolution, many candidates, including George McGovern, believed that those who acted radically would vote against conservatism and for moderate liberalism. What he and others learned is that these people did not vote at all, perhaps believing the whole system corrupt and irrelevant.

The greater error of those who believed they were on the

threshold of total liberation is that the conservative governing order was powerless to meaningfully and vigorously quash a nonviolent cultural revolution and that it lacked the will to do so. In truth many of the towering political leaders of the following decades, such as Richard Nixon and Ronald Reagan, developed their political personalities during the McCarthy era and believed that government simply could not punish enough in defense of traditional culture.

Nixon was the first to act on the knowledge that the politically savvy response to counter-culture mischief and mayhem was to politicize and popularize the cultural role of police as the guardians of orthodox order. This knowledge was practiced in his call in the 1968 election for law and order as a presidential mission, though traditionally issues of crime were under state and local authority. Nixon's campaign manager, Kevin Phillips, in his book *The Emerging Republican Majority* explained that there existed sufficient anger by whites and males and conservatives to create a viable coalition explicitly denouncing the feminist, nonwhite and counter-cultural coalition that had emerged in the liberal era. Thus social conservatism could replace economic conservatism as the centerpiece of Republican politics and achieve a winning coalition to replace the post–Franklin Roosevelt economic ordering of politics.

Kevin Phillips, Richard Nixon and other keen observers of the white middle-class and working-class voter recognized that in response to the Democrat's War on Poverty that a war on drugs and crime was more fitting to a public perception that much of the nation had violated its cherished standards of propriety and was overdue for a good hard lesson in punishment. This political logic translated into a dramatic public policy shift from the liberal-era emphasis on government as helper to the conservative-era emphasis on government as punisher. Both the politics and the policy changes are tied to a philosophical transition from a perception that society's problems are based on poverty, racism, sexism, lack of opportunity and injustice to a view that sin and moral weakness on the part of nonconforming persons is at the heart of all that is ill. In the age of the War on Poverty, it was a concern that criminal law not heighten social injustice. President Johnson's Commission on

Crime concluded that drug abuse policy "often tends to discriminate against the poor and subcultural groups in the population."[16] So criminal law exacerbated injustice. In the logic of the drug war era, bad culture was the root cause of poverty, and so prison coupled with welfare reduction became the essential domestic policy.

President Johnson's Commission on Campus Unrest explored the cultural dimension of marijuana smoking in the context of social conflict and concluded, "If the rest of the society wears short hair, the member of the youth culture wears his hair long. If others are clean, he is dirty. If the others drink alcohol and illegalize marijuana, he denounces alcohol and smokes pot . . . by all these means, he declares himself an alien in a large society with which he is fundamentally at odds." As the cultural challenge of the counter-culture failed, criminalization of their rebellious drug of choice, marijuana, became politically savvy. Drugs became the means to criminalize the culture that challenged dominant orthodoxy.

Nixon acted on this political opportunity. He came to realize that as traditional people saw dirty hippies flouting the rules on sex, drugs and order, they felt incensed even if they had no personal experience in lawlessness. He wrote in 1968, "I have found great audience response to this theme in all parts of the country, including areas like New Hampshire where there is virtually no race problem and relatively little crime."[17] Nixon assigned staff to try to make a connection between recreational drug use and violence and then to publicize such material as a way of organizing political support of his law and order politics. Though illegal drugs as a health concern were minuscule, Nixon recognized the political advantage of deemphasizing use of tobacco and alcohol, lead in pipes and other real health hazards to pound on the culturally advantageous drug issue. Given the small number of users of all other illegal drugs, to have a drug scare with McCarthy-era-like political clout the Nixon administration needed to focus on marijuana. From 1969 to 1971 the number of Americans who reported believing drugs to be the nation's leading problem rose from 3 percent to 23 percent. When Vietnam War peace demonstrators staged a march on Washington in 1971 Nixon seized on the link between marijuana and war protests to order narcotics agents to conduct an early morning raid and incarcerate the crowd. Two weeks later when the director of the National Institute of Mental Health pointed out that medically the criminalization of marijuana was unjustified the president ordered him fired.

Thus when the National Commission on Marihuana and Drug Abuse completed its exhaustive and science-based study and released it under the title *Marihuana, A Signal of Misunderstanding*, they in reality failed to understand the score on marijuana politics. Summarizing the medical data, they concluded that the health effects of the drug are minimal. They also reported that the "gateway drug" theory lacked credibility and that, rather than leading to violence, the smoking of marijuana statistically inhibited such crime. The report continued, "we have grappled with the threshold question: why has the use of marihuana reached problem status in the public mind?" The answer the commission concluded was that, "many see the drug as fostering a counter-culture which conflicts with basic moral precepts, as well as with the operating functions of our society." They explored the deep cultural rejection of marijuana-linked lifestyle choices, including lowered material focus, lowered work importance and lowered sexual inhibition. The drug leads to "rejection of the established value system. . . . Marihuana becomes more than a drug; it becomes a symbol of the rejection of cherished values."

The Nixon-appointed Commission reflected the wisdom of ending this expensive and fundamentally un-American cultural persecution. They concluded,

> Our youth cannot understand why society chooses to criminalize a behavior with so little visible effect or adverse social impact . . . These young people have jumped the fence and found no cliff. And the disrespect for the possession laws fosters a disrespect for law and the system in general. . . . On top of this is the distinct impression among the youth that some police may use the marihuana laws to arrest people they don't like for other reasons, whether it be their politics, their hair style or their ethnic background.[18]

Two decades later a similarly objective panel could not help but include strong recognition of the use of drug laws to impose racial and class oppression. Nixon dismissed the work of his own Commission, and ordered the CIA to enter drug enforcement with the mandate that drug sellers "must be hunted to the end of the earth."

Throughout his career, Nixon confirmed that aggressive use of the police authority can be used to construct and enforce a political majority coalition. As prosecutor before the House Un-American Activities Committee he formed this lesson. He practiced it continuously against communism in the 1950s, and then against the counter-culture in the 1960s. He used this tactic in justifying the National Guard slaying of peace protesters in Kent State and in mass round-ups and lock-ups of protesters in Washington, D.C. He showed how cultural anxiety could be politically harnessed through drug criminalization to great advantage.

The drug war moved from Nixon-era advantage to hard core mass criminalization during the presidency of Ronald Reagan. Reagan became the embodiment of a majoritarian ambition to reset America to its pre-1960s culture. Reagan's rise to political office in California was substantially based on his gifted ability to extol the virtue of intolerance to nonconformists lifestyles and to assemble a coalition based on shared taste for cultural orthodoxy. In the 1966 gubernatorial election he stated that the bad changes to society "began a year ago when the so-called free speech movement advocates, who in truth have no appreciation for freedom, were allowed to assault and humiliate the police, symbol of peace and freedom on campus, and that is the moment when the ringleaders should have been taken by the scruff of the neck and thrown out."[19] His rise to national prominence was fueled by his decision to gas the population of the rebellious Berkeley Campus from a helicopter. In his 1968 presidential bid, the focus of his nomination speech proclaimed that he was the candidate who would confront the rebels with the full force of criminal law. He too learned the political power of prosecutorial politics as an agent for J. Edgar Hoover's FBI assigned to identify communist sympathizers in 1950s Hollywood. Decades later he would act on the belief that the role of criminal law was to save society from changes to national orthodox social order.

In economic policy Reagan advocated deregulation to undo the impact of decades of liberal victories in environmental law, consumer protection law and labor rights. This reduction in government programs matched the administration's rhetoric that "government is the problem" and that the administration would "get government off the back of the people." In social policy he chartered the opposite course, declaring war on the social practices of non-traditional Americans. The sexual revolution came under assault with the attempt to criminalize abortion and restrict access to birth control. Gays found their rights under scrutiny, as did publishers of sexual material. Drug users were aggressively persecuted.

In social policy under the banner of the Reagan Revolution "a cultural civil war" emerged between the "traditionalists and the moderns."[20] The social historian Gary Will summarized, "There is a revolution in social acceptability of all sorts. And various people are caught in the changes and they are in a sense victims in a changed moral world."[21] During the Carter era, women's liberation, the sexual revolution, abortion rights, gay rights, marijuana as a common recreational drug and cocaine as the champagne drug looked as though they had become fixed accepted social realities. Carter recognized that prison was far more expensive and damaging than marijuana and so criminalization of the drug was not good policy or acceptable morality. He and his administration had no mandate or desire to wage cultural war on the hippies and blacks, so rational health and fiscal policy joined with basic values like tolerance, honesty and human decency to become manifest in a reduction of the whole drug issue. On the other frontiers of cultural warfare Carter was at least a passivist, and in many instances he promoted changes in the social and moral structures. He did this despite, or in some ways due to, his genuine religious devotion. His God and Bible were based on love and tolerance and did not call him to the holy domestic crusade practiced by the subsequent administrations.

In the decades after his presidency Carter has devoted himself to service to the poor. The White House took a different direction, launching a series of moral crusades that held the common refrain that poverty is the product of untraditional and bad culture. The War on Drugs is the great manifestation of this punitive focus of domestic public policy. It is linked as social policy with the reduction in welfare, not fully accomplished till the Clinton presidency, the federal war on pornography, the treatment of AIDS as a moral issue rather than a health plague, the Reagan- and Bush-sponsored attempts to criminalize abortion and reduce sexual education in the school systems and the assault on rights gained by gays. These issues helped to crowd the potentially competing concerns of falling quality job opportunity, tax cuts for the wealthy, manipulation of bank failures as a transfer of funds from tax payers to well-connected investors and the continuously rising number of homeless. When President Clinton attempted to change the logic of the conservative era away from punitive government by fostering tolerance for homosexuality and introducing a new focus of national health care, he was clobbered. By returning to the proven formula of profits for the wealthy and prison for the underclass, he stabilized his presidency.

Rejection of the liberationist and progressive policies of the prior liberal era are at the heart of the coalition that held together for the Reagan-Bush terms. In many ways Clinton succeeded for the Democrats because he co-opted the themes of this coalition by adopting many of its policy elements. This is certainly true of use of the drug issue and welfare from Reagan through Clinton. The intervening factor between the promise for human autonomy and social justice in the liberal era and the demand for a more punitive moralist government in the 1980s and 1990s is the Reagan Revolution and its surrounding politics, sociology and jurisprudence. When the Democrats finally overthrew this period of command in the person of Bill Clinton, they echoed similar social policies, thus codifying just how deep the shift in the body politic ran.

Few documents express so poignantly the degree to which assault on unapproved personal choices drove politics as the 1992 National Republican Platform. Among the provisions of this document are a call to comprehensively outlaw all abortions, opposition to all school birth-control counseling and distribution of condoms, support for the ban on homosexuals in the military, opposition to same-sex marriages or adoption by same-sex couples, advocacy of the claim that condoms and clean needles do not help to prevent AIDS and a ban on the sale of *Playboy* magazine at military stores.

To understand how such essentially personal issues came to stand at the focus of public affairs requires consideration of the Reagan coalition. One view of the Reagan coalition is offered by the pollster Norman Orenstein, who suggests that three kinds of conservatives, religious, economic and nationalist, each found in the person of Ronald Reagan their own image.[22] This was a rare political ability on Reagan's part due to the considerable differences among the three conservative types. He blended the three world views of fundamentalism, nationalism and capitalism into a viable whole.

For economic conservatives, there was a sense that government in the prior decades had grown to be a burden on wealth. As Kevin Phillips carefully detailed, the period of the Reagan presidency achieved a massive redistribution of wealth away from the working class and poor to the rich.[23] This has no absolute impact on criminal justice, though as the division between rich and poor expanded, police were called on to enforce the unstable economic order. In addition, the philosophical campaign that the poor exist because of their bad moral character exhibited in drug use and lack of sexual restraint helped to justify a decreased role of government in welfare and an increased use of prisons as the public policy toward the poor.

Nationalist conservatives viewed with alarm weakness showed by the holding of embassy hostages in Iran and the Soviet invasion of Afghanistan. The principle response by the Reagan and Bush administrations was a significant buildup of military armament. In domestic policy, police came to be seen as the essential product of government in nation building. In the early days of Reagan's first term, when every progressive federal program was on the budget chopping block, Budget Director David Stockman suggested trimming the Justice Department work force by 2,000. Attorney General William Smith argued to the President, "The Justice Department is not a domestic agency, it is the internal arm of national defense," to which Reagan agreed, proclaiming "Law enforcement is something we have always believed was a legitimate function of government."[24] An era of the shift of government resources from benevolent deployment to punitive focus had begun. Ultimately the War on Drugs would out-pace the Star Wars orbiting missile system as most expensive federal initiative.

While the nationalist wing and the economic wing of the Republican party benefited from and cooperated in the drug war, it is the religious wing that brought real fervor to the moral crusade to punish a sinful society. Jerry Falwell, leader of the political action group the Moral Majority, said of the 1980 election that it was "the greatest day for the cause of conservatism and American morality in my adult life."[25] Pat Robertson, another leader of the religious right, expressed the passion to rescue the nation from liberal public policy. "The greatest social problem in America is the breakup of the American family," he claimed.[26] Robertson submitted that, "thirty percent of all divorces are caused by welfare laws." He prescribed teaching religious faith in public schools as the cure.

The White House communications director, Pat Buchanan, embraced the agenda of the religious wing of the party and stated that it was policy to promote "the traditional family, that is one in which the wife stays home to take care of the children."[27] Abortion rights, tax policy, education policy, welfare policy and other aspects of government would be used in the effort to restore pre-liberation-era America.

Senator George McGovern recognized the depth of cultural war to be unleashed and stated, "a backlash against social change involving women was the sleeper issue of the 1980s."[28] He explained that "the family issue raised by the right wing was a code word for putting women back in the kitchen, stripping them of any decision on the question of abortion, and forcing them into the old orthodox rules. There was a counter revolutionary aspect to this campaign, and women were the chief victims." In hindsight his comment must be amended. Though the counter-revolution targeted women's rights, gays, blacks and the poor, the users of forbidden drugs were the greatest losers class of all. The demonization of forbidden drugs was at the crux of the conservative era's fervor to restore good traditional social order.

Demographic-based studies add an additional understanding to the era when drug hate dominated American politics and the continuation of the legacy of those politics in policy and administration. Edsal and Edsal argue that politics in America is essentially race based. The Democratic party sided with the civil rights movement to achieve a measure of rights for blacks in the 1960s and has been punished ever since by Southern whites who are traditionalist in race relations. When the Republican party became a majority in the 1980s, it unleashed a new race offensive under the guise of drug policy. Thus mass incarceration has replaced segregation, which replaced slavery as the public policy on race. This theme will be further explored in the next chapter.

A different study of the sociological split between liberals and conservatives is offered by The Post-Modernity Project.[29] Based on the clustering of respondents into similar ideology types researchers find six political personalities. Three lean toward Republican: Traditionalists, Neo-Traditionalists and Conventionalists. Traditionalists are the most socially conservative portion of the Republican coalition and comprise 11 percent of the population. They are overwhelmingly white, fundamentalist Protestants or orthodox Catholics. They believe that the change from what they regard to be traditional morality is the great danger to the nation and undoing those social breaches in order to restore tradition is the essential agenda of public affairs. Most persons in this cluster reached adulthood before the sexual and cultural changes of the 1960s. They are concentrated in the rural Southeast and West Central states. Prior to the Reagan Revolution they did not tend to participate in politics, believing both parties too secular. Since Reagan, they have voted with high frequency and volunteer as grassroots activists in the Republican party.

They are joined by their more educated, more affluent and less evangelic counterparts, the Neo-Traditionalists, in the view that moral failing is the root cause of social problems and that punishment rather than welfare is needed to right social ills. This group, 16 percent of the population, is broader in its sociology, representing more people who matured in the 1960s and 1970s and also is not exclusively white. Conventionalists also can be brought into the "what's wrong with the country is that too many people are doing what ever they please" paradigm, but with them it is mostly a matter of going along with the conservative camp.

At the opposite end of the social and political spectrum are the Permissivists. This is the largest group in the population and is primarily drawn from baby-boomers and Generation Xers. They feel that they have the right to make choices about their lives, and society should learn to tolerate diversity in sexuality and consciousness. Though they are as large as the two most conservative clusters combined, they are not politically engaged. They are liberal in outlook but not inclined to partisan affiliation. Thus at the ideological extremes of American politics, the right actively attempts to criminalize the behavior of the left, and the left fails to fight back in political terms. The War on Drugs is the means by which those who long for the good old days vent their rage against those who have exited the old rules.

Nonparticipation in politics of the Permissivists leaves the final two groups to make the core of the Democratic party. Communitarians and Pragmatists share a willingness for tolerance that makes them compatible with Permissivists, though in their own lives they lean toward traditional behaviors. Communitarians are about 19 percent of the population and believe that the real agenda is to promote the common good through sacrifice and public works. The shift of government from social welfare to moralist disciplinarian is not their agenda. Pragmatists are the most socially diverse of the six clusters. Representing about 14 percent of the population, they believe in religious faith, rather than zeal or holy crusade, that promotes propriety. They believe that positive government is necessary for society to function, but they are skeptical of grand new programs. Though disapproving of homosexuality, pornography and others sins, they overall believe that it is pragmatically best not to legislate against such choices.

Studies suggest insight as to why conservatives have focused so much of their attention on drugs. One scaled 4-year-old children on an index of creativity and adventure seeking to find that such characteristics are the greatest predictor of recreational use of marijuana in subsequent high-school years. Drug users are perhaps by personality disposed to be the least obedient to orthodoxy and convention just as the orthodox are most disposed to believe that social rules must be reinforced with persecution of the non-conformists. Conflict over drug use is the great continuation of the unending dialectic between what Freud called anal retentive personalities and their natural opponents, the oral compulsives. Rule lovers are in a constant effort to bring rule breakers to task, while rule breakers seek new horizons for their will to creative non-conformity.

The creative and gregarious side of drug use was exposed in San Francisco's Haight Ashbury neighborhood in the 1960s and in the many subsequent little life-style-free zones that spread across the country. With the LSD-based psychedelic revolution, new music, new visual art, new drama in the form of performance art and an array of other expressions exploded into popular culture. Psychological study of the heavily LSD-using population showed that they had changed in what was labeled the means-to-life index, preferring time for reflection and creative self-expression to traditional acquisition of material goods as a life goal.[30]

Ronald Reagan gave clear voice to the view that the drug culture stood guilty of contaminating the larger society and must be neutralized and punished. For traditionalists looking to restore pre-1960s culture, he showed how by focusing on forbidden drug use as crime; the era of the 1960s could be disparaged and the counter-culture incarcerated. In 1986 he stated that "the gurus of hedonism and permissiveness of the 1960s and 1970s who shared a flippant and irresponsible attitude toward drug use" are responsible. "Drug users can no longer excuse themselves by blaming society. The rest of us must be clear that while we are sympathetic, we will no longer tolerate the use of illegal drugs by anyone."[31] George Bush's Drug Czar Bob Martinez continued the theme that in essence the drug war was about the stomping out of wrong culture. He asserted that the major obstacle to success of the government's offensives is the continued existence of persons "thirty-five years and older who grew up with the wrong cultural inputs." An orthodoxy solidified that the drug culture and its many correlations as counter-cultures were the enemy of traditional order. William Bennett as Drug Czar and prophet of religious virtue expressed the identity of the drug war best. As Secretary of Education, he argued that the "cultural war" must be fought against "bilingual education, multiculturalism and the chasing of God from the classroom." As Drug Czar he proclaimed that there was no need to consider the public health or public safety costs of the drug war because "the simple fact is drug use is wrong. And the moral argument in the end is the most compelling argument."[32]

Drug hate is thus the greatest contemporary manifestation of the ageless dialectical conflict between those who support traditional culture and those who seek fundamental change to the larger culture through self-liberation. The orthodox order has many means at its command. First among these certainly is deployment of the power of punishment to neutralize contesting individuals and their community. The War on Drugs has seen deployment of this prime power on a scale unmatched in the nation's history. Other powers have also contributed to the smashing of the counter-culture. These include rhetoric by politicians who recognized a vast harnessable reservoir of disdain by the Traditionalists against the various forms of new culture, use to the media which in the 1980s became drug war beneficiaries and enthusiasts, and use of class and race consciousness as weapons to uphold the traditional order. All of these factors are explored in the next chapter.

NOTES

1. Jonathan Shedler and Jack Block, "Adolescent Drug Use and Psychological Health: A Longitudinal Inquiry," *American Psychologist* (May 1990), 612.

2. Arnold Trebach and Kevin Zeese, *Drug Prohibition and the Conscience of Nations* (Washington, D.C., The Drug Policy Foundation, 1990), p. 29.

3. "Study Finds Drug Users' Role In Gun Crimes is Exaggerated," *New York Times*, Oct. 8, 1995.

4. Louis Harris & Associates and Alan F. Westin, *The Dimensions of Privacy* (New York and London, Garland, 1981).
5. James Miller, *The Passion of Michel Foucault* (New York, Simon and Schuster, 1993).
6. Sigmund Freud, *Civilization and Its Discontents* (New York and London, W. W. Norton, 1961).
7. Robert Griffith, *The Politics of Fear* (Amherst, University of Massachusetts Press, 1987).
8. David Rosenbloom, *Public Administration and the Law*: Bench v. Bureau *in the United States* (New York, Mercel Dekker, 1983).
9. Robert MacNeil, *The Way We Were: 1963 The Year Kennedy was Shot* (New York, Carrol and Graph, 1988), 26.
10. Bashey Heath, *John F. Kennedy: Profiles in Courage* (New York, Taurus Press, 1973).
11. Charles Perry, *The Haight-Ashbury* (New York, Vintage, 1985).
12. Ronald Siegel, *Intoxication* (New York, E. P. Dutton, 1989).
13. Alfred Kinsey, *Sexual Behavior and the Human Male* (Philadelphia, Saunders, 1948).
14. Jay Stevens, *Storming Heaven: LSD and the American Dream* (New York, Atlantic Monthly Press, 1987), 279.
15. Charles Reich, *The Greening of America* (New York, Bantam Books, 1970), 281.
16. Dan Baum, *Smoke and Mirrors* (Boston, Little Brown, 1996), 7.
17. Ibid., p. 11.
18. John Orman, *The Politics of Rock Music* (Chicago, Nelson Hall, 1984), p. 56.
19. David Sadofsky, *The Question of Privacy in Public Policy* (Westport, CT: Praeger, 1993), 3.
20. "Cultural Civil War: Permissive 60's Generation," *New York Times*, Nov. 9, 1987.
21. "Ginsburg Episode Revives Discord of the 60's Generation," *New York Times*, Nov. 8, 1987.
22. Norman Orenstein, *The People, the Press, and Politics: The Times-Mirror Study of the American Electorate* (Reading, MA, Addison-Wesley, 1988).
23. Kevin Phillips, *The Politics of Rich and Poor* (New York, Random House, 1990).
24. Dan Baum, *Smoke and Mirrors* (Boston, Little Brown, 1996), 138.
25. "Dispute on Religion Raised by Campaign," *New York Times*, Nov. 9, 1980.

26. Ibid.
27. Ibid.
28. "Feminists Dismayed by the Election and Unsure of What the Future Holds," *New York Times*, Nov. 7, 1980.
29. James Hunter and Carl Bowman, *The Post-Modernity Project* (New York, Gallup Organization, 1997).
30. Jay Stevens, *Storming Heaven*.
31. "Reagan Considers Wider Drug Testing," *New York Times*, July 31, 1986.
32. Dan Baum, *Smoke and Mirrors*, p. 264.

5

Winners in the War on Drugs

The scale of the War on Drugs is immense and the irrationality profound. Surely the War on Drugs is the greatest modern reminder that policy is the product of politics and cultural forces rather than of a rational cost-benefit analysis. For a society to inflict such deep wounds upon itself the political, social and economic forces and their alignment must run deep. Again, over a third of all state prisoners are serving time for drug offenses, while less than a fifth were convicted of violent crimes. The majority of federal prisoners are incarcerated for drugs. Marijuana, a drug far safer than either tobacco or alcohol, heads the list as cause of incarceration. The FBI's Uniform Crime Report estimated 588,963 marijuana arrests in 1995 to achieve over 1.5 million marijuana arrests in the first three years of the Clinton presidency. Criminal justice in America, the fastest growing field of the public sector, is more about forbidden sin than crimes against persons or property. While not reducing drug use, the public sector has shifted funding priorities from all the programs that are meant to help people and build the quality of life to punishment of crimes against cultural sins. Consider these vignettes of the era.

George Bush, seeking reelection, announced in 1992 that Homestead Air Base, destroyed by hurricane and previously slated for closure, would be rebuilt. Its new mission in post–cold war deployment would be as military barrier against drug smuggling. He proposed $1 billion to restore and refit a base for this mission. Meanwhile drug smugglers simply switched to vehicles crossing from Mexico to avoid air and sea challenges. So by 1997 relations with Mexico, a neighbor with an array of legitimate diplomatic concerns, were dominated by drug traffic.

On the Mexico-Texas border the national tradition of keeping the military out of domestic police affairs has been sacrificed. In May, 1996, Marines on a drug patrol shot and killed an 18-year-old boy out herding his goats. Though no evidence was presented that he was a part of the drug trade in nearby Roma, Texas, the authorities decided that most of the town might be complicit. Seventy-nine people were arrested in December, 1996, and charged with marijuana smuggling. All of the persons arrested were poor; most could not afford to hire a lawyer for their defense.[1] Remaining residents said, during an interview, that if they spoke out in any way they feared retaliation, either from the real drug smugglers or from the law enforcement authorities. Residents explained that the county is very poor, among the poorest in the nation. Some people may have been drawn into the drug trade to feed their kids and pay for food. The government seemed willing to pay anything for prisons, prosecutors, military patrols and drug agents, but nothing for housing, medical care or food.

In Arizona, the town of Cleopatra Hill was rejuvenated as traditional locals and counter-culture arrivals discovered that by respecting each other's privacy, both communities became viable. Sergeant Alan Schmidt of the town's police department summarized, "It's a town that would like to secede and carry on its own lifestyle. The people there strongly believe in an individual's freedom above all else."[2] Success of the town ended with a dawn raid as 100 federal and state agents descended to arrest the chief of police, the mayor and members of the city council. Women and children were dragged from their beds as many of the citizens of the town were rounded up for arrest. As

America searched in the 1980s for the restoration of alleged traditional culture, counter-culture enclaves were ripe for demonstrative punishment.

In Hawking, Texas, the town decided to change the rules for participation in school-sponsored extracurricular activities. All children in grades six through twelve were required to submit to urine drug testing before being allowed to participate. Thus many of the children who would most benefit from a structured sport experience were precluded from registration by fear of arrest. Drug-testing programs spread through the nation, teaching children the irrelevance of the Constitutional promise.

At sea, the pleasure craft *Ark Royal* and the research vessel *Atlantis II* were seized. The pleasure craft was found to have ten seeds and two stems of marijuana plants. The research vessel contained .01 of an ounce of marijuana in a crew member's shaving kit. Similarly, in Florida, David Phelps lost his shrimp boat when the Coast Guard found three grams of stems and seeds on board. Thus a profitable pattern was set to be repeated hundreds of times and formed an aspect of the answer to the question of who benefits in America from this public policy disaster. For the seizing agencies, war plunder proved immensely profitable.

New York City's Mayor Koch invoked a novel plan to escalate the domestic war. The city began to demolish tenement apartments in designated drug neighborhoods, particularly in upper Manhattan. The justification for this assault on the housing stock of the poor was the truthful assertion that no amount of arrests of impoverished persons for narcotic trade reduced the flow of drugs. New unemployed youths always entered the trade to replace the incarcerated dealers. Cheap apartments, alternatively, were in limited supply. Demolition cleared out the old neighborhood, thereby making way for upscale condominiums. No consideration of where the displaced families might move was made. The use of the drug war in class rivalry is another of the factors of its political viability.[3]

In Montana, the Kurth family, faced with foreclosure on the family farm, turned to marijuana cultivation. Although the Kurths were two bank payments away from solvency, the state seized the farm. The profitability of such seizures has not escaped the notice of local police and further adds to the politics of the war.

In Oklahoma, the sheriff of Marrietta and one of his officers were arrested for plotting to illegally cross state lines and kidnap a man with the intent of bringing him back to their jurisdiction and subjecting him to torture. Their intent was to achieve an inquisition-style confession from the man that he dealt drugs. The town rose up in outrage so the plan was frustrated. The president of a local bank commented, "The Country has been talking about the drug problem, and here is a man trying to do something." Unmitigated allegiance to the drug war has become a new kind of aggressive patriotism, replacing communism as the socially acceptable and personally satisfying form of hate.

In Virginia, three fraternities were raided and eleven students arrested at the University of Virginia. The police chief stated, "Up there in academia they're not always living in the real world. The students had gotten to where they thought they could do anything they wanted." Flirtation of the idea of self-liberating freedom by university students and the vigorous rejection of such claims by socially conservative America is the root history of the drug war.

In Southern Florida, an officer of the DEA warned that drug trafficking is so central to the regional economy that after the agency eliminates smuggling, "Dade County is going to be in for one hell of a recession."[4] In fact the agent could not have been more wrong. Dade County first enjoyed immense federal target funds in the form of bases to corridor off the coast, and never did without its vital trade and money transfer banking. Customs Commissioner William Von Raab submitted that the war effort must only be judged in terms of quantity seized, which was immense, rather than elimination or reduction of markets, which proved too resilient.

In California, the state suffered in the early 1990s under a deficit that reached $11 billion in 1992. Education, social services, health and public lands budgets were all slashed. Only one program managed to grow under these conditions. Expenditures on prisons reached an all-time high. Cultivation of marijuana, the state's most valuable crop, and urban drug sales led the causes for incarceration. By the summer of 1997 the federal government was spending millions of dollars annually to send military helicopters over rural mountainous counties in an attempt to eradicate outdoor marijuana cultivation. It is the topic of this chapter to consider the use of the drug war in shifting funds away from liberal social spending, as well as the political use of heightened incarceration of the culturally divergent and the popularity of widespread incarceration of minority youths.

The racial politics of the drug war were played out graphically in the nation's capital. Determined to score a public relations victory, Drug Czar William Bennett and President Bush decided to target full federal resources to prove once and for all that raw unfettered police power could break drug use. After building massive prisons and spending billions of dollars, they instead proved that politicians can yield political benefit without achieving any substantive policy result. The White House labeled the campaign "Operation Clean Sweep." The National Guard and, of more importance, the national press corp were deployed in a mass incarceration publicity effort. Use of the war to press and politicians is at the heart of explaining the profitability of the war. Bennett in particular expressed the linkage of the war to an overall cultural and religious offensive.

The Rand Corporation in reviewing Operation Clean Sweep concluded, "The Washington area problem for heroin, PCP, and cocaine is worse than that of most comparable metropolitan areas. There is, unfortunately, little to suggest that enforcement has had many of the intended consequences."[5] The federal government inflicted on the city an incarceration rate over five times the national average per capita, substantially higher than the next highest cities of Baltimore, New York and Los Angeles. It imposed harsh prison sentences on the mostly black population, averaging 39 months for each drug conviction, one-third longer than the national average.

The glaring realities of Operation Clean Sweep are that white official Washington conducted a mass criminalization against black residential Washington. This operation attracted major television and other media coverage with daily footage of live-action drug war maneuvers. Politicians reaped reward until the absence of benefit became too glaring. Then Mayor Barry, the occasionally drug using though popular and progressive black mayor, was set up to switch the political dynamics.

Perhaps the most graphic reminder of the logic of the drug war was presented in a press conference in 1997. There, General Barry McCaffrey, dressed in full military uniform and serving under President Clinton as Drug Czar, instructed the editors of the *New England Journal of Medicine* and doctors of the American Medical Association that there was no valid medical evidence of the value of marijuana. The *New England Journal of Medicine* had recently published its finding to the contrary, as had the National Institutes of Health. The general has no medical training. But his findings to the contrary of the elite medical science institutions needed none. The drug war is based on loyalty to orthodoxy; the general knew there to be no science supporting the value of marijuana as a simple application of his patriotism. He and many others needed no further study.

These vignettes depict the elements of an understanding of the support for this policy area. The War on Drugs can be understood by examination of the value of the campaign to politicians, the media, cultural chauvinism, furtherance of racism, class conflict and institutional advantage. It is by adding each of these beneficiaries and considering the interlocking agendas thus formed that America's insane domestic war can be understood as in its own way rational.

Though Nixon was the first modern President to explore the strategic electoral advantage of fostering drug hate, it was Ronald Reagan who dominated the field. The source of Reagan's advantage is precisely that for Nixon domestic cultural war was a calculated tactic to criminalize his left-wing opposition and deflect attention away from the Vietnam War, while for Reagan drug hate was a natural and consistent portion of his personality, world view and experience. Drug hate also fit precisely into his image as conservative warrior and served to cement his cumbersome conservative coalition. All these factors together help to explain how drug hate became the essential political phenomenon of his conservative administration. The Reagan presidency and the conservative era of the 1980s cannot be well understood without focusing on the deployment and success of drug hate as a movement and phenomena.

U.S. News and World Report was early to recognize the potency of the use of narcotics as a moral crusade to change the political order. In 1986 they editorialized that

> easily the most prominent beneficiary of the drug furor is Ronald Reagan. Just weeks ago the president seemed trapped in a thicket of thorny problems. For now at least, all that has been changed. Other issues have not gone away, but they have been pushed to the back burner, providing Reagan with much needed breathing room and a chance to do what he does best—rouse the troops in a campaign summoning the traditional American values so key to his popularity.[6]

Issues of the economy, abortion, growing deficit and the super expensive Strategic Defense Initiative divided and so weakened the Reagan coalition. Drugs proved remarkably useful at distracting political attention from real issues and focusing attention instead on a moralism that reinforced a broad conservative order.

For the traditional economic conservatives the drug war offered an excuse to eliminate the array of Great Society programs that were designed to end poverty. In accordance with drug hate ideology, poverty was no longer to be viewed as a matter of social injustice, racism, gender barriers, and limited opportunity and education. Failure in American society was instead the result of bad culture and poor moral development as exhibited in taste for forbidden illicit drug pleasures. Spending money on people who indulged in a forbidden pleasure was a waste since they would only misuse any opportunity. The role of government thus could shift away from the despised welfare agenda to the appreciated criminal justice system. Government no longer worked to limit income equality; it served to advance it through punishment of the wretched. An expanded criminal justice system helped to stabilize an economy that fostered increasing disparity between the rich and poor. Enhanced prison and police systems were ready for deployment if the poor attempted redistribution in a criminal manner.

For nationalist conservatives the War on Drugs meant an active role for the armed services in the wake of peace initiatives with the traditional Soviet enemy. Men in uniform, rather than suffering the general reduction of government in an era of domestic budget cuts, could be deployed against the cultural enemy within. With the relaxation of *pax comitatus*, barring use of the military on American soil for the first time in the nation's history the military services were free to actively engage in domestic affairs. Through an array of laws the federal government and its resources moved from the sidelines to the center of domestic police work. The federal government took the lead in pressing for increased police power deployed to the conservative cultural campaign. Most fundamentally, in an age that lacked a quality enemy, drug hate gave meaning to nationalist patriotism. A world without an evil enemy is a world without moral compass to those who define themselves as warrior. Between the era of the fall of the Berlin Wall and the rise of Iraq as substitute "evil empire," drug hate played an especially meaningful role.

For religious conservatives the War on Drugs was the great modern application of puritanic theology in public affairs. Sin would be punished by government for the benefit of the righteous. Here as well drug hate was a means of affirmation of the growing dominance of Southern white male demographic rule over northern liberal secular and ethnic leadership that had previously prospered.

Jerry Falwell, a Southern Baptist preacher and leader of the religious-based political pressure group the Moral Majority said that the election of Reagan to replace Jimmy Carter was "the greatest day for the cause of conservatism and American morality in my adult life."[7] Much of the religious right's agenda would go unfulfilled. But a crackdown on illicit vice, from drugs to pornography and homosexuality, was the portion of the moralist mandate Reagan could act on. Religious denunciation of sin translated into public policy by transforming criminal justice from a force primarily for public safety to a force primarily about cultural control and the forced adherence to the rules of orthodox order.

The *New Republic*, in an article entitled "Reverend Reagan," attempted to describe the theology which made the political core of Reaganism.[8] To Reagan, they argued, history had reached its climax. America was the embattled nation of the biblical book Revelations. It faced an external enemy in the Soviet Union and a domestic foe of the bad 1960s spawned culture disdainfully labeled secular humanism. He viewed himself as the President at war with both forces.

To fight this offensive within the nation, his administration advanced what came to be called a pro-family agenda to combat what the President declared as "two liberal decades that had frayed the fabric of the nation's moral structure." Reduction in two-parent households, Reagan submitted, was the cause of drug use and crime. He linked drugs back to the focal religious issue of abortion rights by reasoning that those who opposed the banning of abortion were "responsible for the decline in respect for human life" that led to social decay and self-indulgence.[9]

Reagan declared 1983 the "Year of the Bible" and condemned the "expulsion of God from the classroom." He asserted that the Bible contained the answer to all of the world's problems and claimed the separation of government and religion to be the reason government had pursued bad liberal policies instead of morally grounded punitive policies.

The leadership of the religious right thus easily allied itself with Reagan. At the 1984 Republican National Convention, Jerry Falwell was called as a speaker. He released a "Biblical Scoreboard" to compare the virtue of Ronald Reagan with that of Walter Mondale. Reagan definitively won divinely scriptured endorsement. A different, but related alliance was formed with the Vatican and Catholic hierarchy. Pope John Paul and President Ronald Reagan agreed about the need to force conservative values, including abortion, homosexuality, traditional gender roles and a condemnation of many pleasures of the flesh as sin.

President Carter, a genuine born-again Christian, lost contact with the rising force of conservative politicized evangelism.

He declared during the 1980 campaign that "in our country we ought to be able to separate church and state." He further stated, "My religious beliefs are very precious to me and I have never tried to criticize those who worshiped differently from me. But until this year I have never had anyone question the sincerity of my religious belief in god."

Reagan was unable to deliver a large portion of his agenda. Though he scaled back aid to the poor, there was always sufficient Democratic control of the legislature to preclude more than incremental reduction until the Clinton presidency when Republicans took control of the legislature and a new Democratic policy held sway in the White House. Despite considerable effort, significant legal restriction of abortion also proved illusive because of voter, congressional and judicial opposition. In the regulatory context there proved to be real limits to the agenda to eliminate environmental protection. Republican polling data revealed by 1996 that the majority of voting Republicans wanted no reduction in environmental protection.

In deployment of the criminal justice system against undesired culture Reagan discovered his most politically achievable domestic arena. There is a considerable population-based defense of most sin as defined and denounced by religious orthodoxy. Homosexuality and abortion have shown particularly widespread and vigorous support groups. Gambling, alcohol and tobacco all have financial and institutional defenders willing to confront moralist attacks. Tobacco production and distribution are too demographically synonymous with the core of the socially conservative right to form an acceptable foe. Illegal drugs, pornography and some nonconformist sexualities do not enjoy formidable defense groups. And so an administration anxious to conduct a campaign on sin was well advised to make drugs and pornography the central offensives.

Religious Reaganism in the United States can also be seen as a portion of a world sociological event. Martin Marty, editor of the *Fundamentalist Project*, explains that the 1970s were a period in which fundamentalists began to assert themselves politically after being dormant since the 1930s. Around the world, among Jews, Christians and Muslims, religious orthodoxy took to politics in defense of the old ways and in response to the threat of liberating secularism and hedonistic consumerism.

In America, the particular rise of political power among fundamentalists is due to a blending of modern technology, including computers and television, with deeply held antimodern devotion to sociology of the past. Fundamentalists found mass media, mass education and much of liberal public policy threatening to their ability to live in isolation from the profane larger culture. As they recognized that it was impossible to control local television, movie theaters, textbook production or art displays through local politics, they asserted themselves in national politics in an attempt to control culture. Mass culture had penetrated their lives promoting liberated sexuality, a diversity of forms of intoxication and an array of forbidden choices. They fought back and ultimately declared a criminal justice war against sinful culture.

Jerry Falwell and Pat Robertson in particular used access to controlled media and direct political influence to lobby for limitation of freedoms granted in the liberal era. Opposition to the Equal Rights Amendment, gay rights and abortion rights led their list. Drug hate and the need to eliminate drug culture was a staple of their programming and agenda.

Beyond fundamentalist religious circles drug hate became a cultural and political movement in much the way that drug use and drug culture was both personal and political in the prior era. Drug hate enthusiasts formed clubs to celebrate their status. These included PRIDE (Parent Resource Institute for Drug Education), "DARE" (Drug Awareness Resistance Education) and "Just Say No." These clubs held conventions and parties as any social unit might. They produced literature, sought extended membership and became meaningful causes for many of their activists. As drug use in the prior decades was a reaction to the conformity and sterility of the larger culture, so too in the 1980s and 1990s drug hate seemed to hold an important social meaning. Perhaps this was a manifestation of longing for simpler times when the gender roles were more defined, morality more absolute, white culture more dominant and American power more certain. It is a powerful sociological event that in the decade after "sex, drugs and rock and roll" as an anthem of a generation, a different anthem of "Just Say No" took hold. Drug hate is about as focal to understanding society and politics in the conservative era as drug love is to understanding the prior liberal era.

Baseball, the nation's pastime, was inevitably drawn into the sociological phenomenon. It is difficult to imagine greater disproof of the claimed disabling effects of drugs than that elite athletes can engage in recreational use of drugs and yet perform in complex competitive situations with such precision that enemies of drugs and their forbidden pleasures demanded urine testing to determine who to target. Yet in the age of popularized drug hate, the baseball commissioner ordered "everyone from owner down" to submit to invasive testing.[10] That the commissioner had no legal authority to enforce such a ruling among the owners and professional staff was not relevant to the popularity of carrying out a mission of drug hate during the Reagan era. This pattern of assault on the rights of suspected non-conforming populations was carried out in other industries, from railroads to college athletics. As the prior hate movement known as McCarthyism legitimated the search for ideological non-conformists in media, academia and labor unions, the War on Drugs legitimated broad cultural uses of coercive authority that enforced dominance relationships.

Ronald Reagan more than any other person set the stage for this politically beneficial sweeping hate movement. In his 1982 War on Drugs kickoff address he announced, "We've taken down the surrender flag and run up the battle flag."[11] He informed the listeners that he was taking the country into a state of domestic warfare; "we're making no excuses for drugs—hard, soft or otherwise. Drugs are bad and we're going after them and we are going to win the War on Drugs." The President and his wife announced that a "bold confident plan" for eradication would soon be announced with Vice-president Bush in command of a special task force to press engagement off the coast of Florida using the combined police and military might of the nation. The President called for more prosecutors, police and military deployment. He boasted that already the program should be judged an initial success, as measured by a 40 percent increase in persons incarcerated and an 80 percent increase in marijuana seized.

This honest and instructive address marks the beginning of the current hardcore War on Drugs. With the economy failing, much of the conservative social agenda blocked in Congress, and Reagan trailing both Walter Mondale and Ted Kennedy in the polls, a bold strategy using the power of the presidency and Ronald Reagan's gift to sell cultural conservatism proved an ideal strategy. Reagan trumpeted the need for a mass hate. The masses and many elite institutions such as the media and armed services joined in.

Reagan kept the rhetorical heat on for the rest of his administration with phrases such as, "a national crusade against drugs, a sustained, relentless effort to rid America of this scourge by mobilizing every segment of society against drug abuse,"[12] "Drug abuse is a repudiation of everything America is. The destructiveness and human wreckage mock our heritage," "Drug users can no longer excuse themselves by blaming society. The rest of us must be clear that while we are sympathetic, we no longer tolerate the use of illegal drugs by anyone." He claimed, "Our commitment to this program is unshakable: we intend to do what is necessary to end the drug menace and cripple organized crime. We live at a turning point, one of those critical eras in history when time and circumstances unite with sound instinct of good and decent people to make a crucial difference in the lives of future generations."[13] Ronald Reagan, with conviction and rhetorical vigor, invited Americans to measure patriotism by the quality of their drug hate much as three decades earlier anti-communism was the credential of nationalism. As one of the classic political moves, Reagan successfully scapegoated a helpless minority for the benefit of organizing the majority.

With his success others learned the value of drug hate. Not least of these was his own successor, George Bush. The business community broadly learned the value of drug policy in reminding workers of who the powerful are, local governments and the military learned the budget advantages of a drug war as federal funds and forfeiture money became abundantly available for the plucking. Deputy Attorney General Edward C. Schmults summarized the place of the drug war machine in public policy for the era:

> We've had the largest percentage increase in dollars and people of any major agency in the Government including the Department of Defense. We've gone up one billion dollars, darn near fifty percent and most of it has gone to law enforcement. This is a significant and dramatic increase, reflecting the Administration's commitment to law enforcement. It's not rhetoric, it's there. In the Carter Administration Justice was considered just another part of domestic budget. But now there is a recognition of justice as the agency which delivers domestic defense.[14]

Reagan restored the notion that the job of government was to protect society from the enemy within, particularly sin and cultural deviance, rather than to promote the public's welfare. Incarceration rather than income support, prisons rather than public housing, parole officers rather than social workers, this was the ideology and policy that came to hold sway. A national assault on sin became the mechanism for comprehensive budget reform and a shift in the fundamental nature of government from helper to punisher.

President Reagan coherently summarized the use of the War on Drugs as a lever to shift the fundamental ideology behind government away from liberalism. In a 1982 address delivered to the Justice Department, he declared of liberalism that

> at the root of this philosophy lies utopian presumptions about human nature that see man as primarily a creature of his material environment. By changing this environment through expensive social programs, this philosophy holds that government can permanently change man and usher in an era of prosperity and virtue. In much the same way, individual wrongdoing is seen as the result of poor socioeconomic conditions or an underprivileged background.

In short, "society not the individual is to blame."[15]

Reagan then proceeded to reject the idea that society bore any responsibility for sin, violence or poverty. He claimed all would be well if individuals only knew "that right and wrong do matter, that individuals are responsible for their actions." That sense of responsibility could only be provided by punishment of forbidden conduct. Thus government is justified in the criminalization of sin as crime and owes no duty to the disadvantaged other than to serve as moralist punisher. The War on Drugs successfully replaced the Great Society as national plan.

Yet the war did not only seek to punish the sins of the losing class alone. Every recipient of financial aid to higher education was forced to sign their abstinence pledges. Over 3 million upwardly educated Americans have done so. None are known to have declined. There is a $10,000 fine and 1-year prison term for false statements. Statistically, over 1 million Americans have been placed in criminal jeopardy by these requirements. When students protested this government-imposed trap at the University of California at Berkeley, the Justice Department deployed photographers to establish the identity of such disloyalty.

The Reagans gave the nation a whole vocabulary by which to justify the new patriotism of drug hate. "Narco-terrorism" justified dealing with drugs as evil. Program names such as "Zero Tolerance," "Operation Smash," "Operation Invincible" and "Operation Hammer" all reflected this mentality of domestic cultural war in which questions of constitutionality, morality and public policy utility would be suppressed in favor of patriotic and religious zeal. It was Nancy Reagan in particular who introduced the rhetoric that parents should view drug use by children as a statement of defiance of parental authority. She submitted that parents should assume drug use when children "become combative, secretive, and unable to get along with the family."[16] She recommended that all rebelliousness by teenagers be seen as prelude to drug use and that the "toughlove" technique was the kind of discipline parents needed to learn. The home must join the state in deploying authority to squash deviance.

As psychedelics were not the only revolution of the liberal era, so too the War on Drugs was not the only criminal justice initiative launched to eliminate bad culture in the conservative era. The sexual revolution was a significant portion of the 1960s, and there was a genuine backlash to the lowering of sexual rules in the 1980s.

In 1970 the federal government assembled a team of academicians to study the social impact of viewing sexually explicit material. They released a report, entitled *The Presidential Commission Report of Obscenity and Pornography*, which concluded that there was no evidence that the viewing of pornography could be tied to antisocial behavior. Accordingly they recommended comprehensive legalization. In the 1980s with the conservative will to restructure society through punishment and the Reagan administration's will to increase the role of government as cultural police force, these findings and direction were reversed. They convened a new commission which they believed could be stacked to achieve the opposite result by selecting law enforcement professionals rather than wrong-minded academicians to analyze the data. Attorney General Edwin Meese vowed, before the panel was even seated, to launch an "all out campaign against the distribution of obscene material."[17]

Controversy surrounding the Meese Commission offers a case study on the extent to which the conservative punishment movement was willing to go to redeem this sinful nation. The Justice Department used the report process to intimidate retail outlets to cease distribution of *Playboy* and other such magazines. The Commission sent, on Justice Department stationery, letters to store managers stating that they had "received testimony alleging that your company is involved in the sale or distribution of pornography" and hence was subject to prosecution. The Justice Department knew that such prosecution was unconstitutional. As in the War on Drugs, in the Meese Commission simple honesty gave way to a view of a higher morality based on saving the nation from forbidden sin. It took a federal district court order to force the Commission to send a letter of retraction. The court further ordered the Commission not to publish or continue its list of targeted distributors. The general counsel to the American Booksellers Association commented, "this is the kind of conduct one might expect from organized crime or from a totalitarian dictatorship, not from an official agency of the United States Government."[18] *Playboy*'s spokesperson said, "The First Amendment stands between Americans and the prejudice of moral vigilantes in and out of government."[19]

The Commission switched tactics but maintained the objective of criminalizing sin in order to redeem culture. The Commission released a report that claimed an objective basis for a conclusive linkage between the consumption of pornography and antisocial behavior. In keeping with punitive ideology, they called for mandatory prison sentencing, seizure of assets, reinterpretation of the law to criminalize the actors as practitioners of prostitution, and the creation of an agency within the Justice Department to conduct prosecutions.

Unfortunately for the Commission, many of the authorities whose work they cited could not abide by the falsified results of the document. Dissenting members also registered their objection, stating that the report's "proof of a causal link . . . simply cannot be accepted." One of the researchers called the report "bizarre." Upon review of the whole document, researchers concluded that it was "little more than prudishness and moralizing masquerading behind social science jargon." Nevertheless, 8,000 retail outlets ceased to carry the magazines under the unlawful pressure. The media director for Christian Voice concluded, "the Justice Department should be commended for stepping forward to point out the negative effects pornography has on our society. Pornographic material has been shown to be a cause of child abuse and sexually oriented crimes. Hopefully, this report will make headway in eliminating the plague of pornographic pollution which has ravaged our society."[20]

More sad fruit of the Meese Commission's work became public years later as it was exposed that the postal inspector had poured through mail lists to discover the identity of persons who purchased through the mail magazines depicting nudes. Through the creation of dummy corporations with such names as "The American Hedonist Society" and "Heartland Institute for a New Tomorrow," which ran advertisements that tricked citizens into ordering material, the government attempted to identify and punish the impure. Two such unfortunates committed suicide rather than face the social stigma of public revelation of their homosexual viewing selections. Finally, one victim filed suit and had these tactics declared illegal as entrapment. Cynically, the advertisements sent out to entrap these persons contained the claim that ordering through these associations was a way to fight government "hysterical nonsense" and preserve the First Amendment right to view and read freely.

Edwin Meese continued to assert that the government was "committed to redoubling the federal effort to insure that those criminal elements who are trafficking in obscenity are pursued with a vengeance and prosecuted to the hilt."[21] He called for the criminalization of phone and cable television pornography.

Tens of millions of Americans consume sexual entertainment. The Internet has increased both the ease and variety of sexual communications. The business in all its forms is intertwined throughout the economy and society. The implications of the assault on pornography rivals the War on Drugs in political anatomy and policy implication. Millions of Americans deeply disapprove of the behavior of millions of other Americans. A nation with less of a puritanic streak might have the wisdom to live and let live. Americans instead criminalize each other yet violate the law in their own personal lives. There is no greater reason to believe that this criminalization would succeed where Prohibition and the War on Drugs failed. There is much reason to believe both that the moralist constituency would applaud the attempt no matter how unsuccessful it proved and that increased criminal activity and government expenditure would be part of the objective public policy failure. Thousands of people might have their lives ruined through incarceration without any real return to the nation if the courts had not balked at this irrational and unconstitutional use of criminal justice authority.

The attempt to criminalize abortion is an even greater focus of the conservative will to use police power to correct this errant society. Unlike drug policy, liberal political figures exercised their ideological convictions to block widespread criminalization of abortion. Indeed, abortion as an issue is probably the most vocalized confrontation between advocates of traditional, theologically based punitive morality and modern, humanistic-based tolerance morality.

As the Reagan-Bush administrations transformed pre-existing drug policies into the ferocity of the War on Drugs, so too the pre-existing abortion politics were ratcheted up into a national conflict. Opposition to legal abortion became a focal piece of the Republican National Platform. The public policy implications of a drug war–style War on Abortion are staggering. The act is performed on over 1 million Americans annually. All the reasons of the failure of the drug war, war on pornography and prohibition come into play. Though some women will obey the new culturally derived criminal code, many, perhaps most, would not. So there would be mass non-compliance, demanding ever harsher and greater police enforcement. Civil liberties would come under assault as police found the rules of the Constitution a barrier to winning the abortion war. Hence the legitimacy of government and its domestic institutions of police, courts and prisons would be undermined. Meanwhile the expense of this punitive focus would drain resources that could have been used to raise the quality of life and could have perhaps led to people making better life decisions and needing fewer abortions. Illegally administered abortion services meanwhile would sprout an unregulated black-market with an array of costs to society. Penalties all the while would escalate as conservative politics demanded greater control of this sinful nation through punishment. As in all the many other failed attempts to remold society through the infliction of pain, politicians would deploy rhetoric to hide the fact that much punishment actually translates into little change of the targeted personal behavior.

Ronald Reagan deployed his flair for rhetoric that raised angry intolerance to a chauvinistic righteousness in the abortion issue. In 1986 Reagan stated, “I don’t think that I’m trying to do something that is taking a privilege away from womanhood, because I don’t think that womanhood should be considering murder to be a privilege.”[22] He condemned in 1983, “the excruciating pain the unborn must feel as their lives are snuffed out.”

In that same speech he declared 1983 to be the Year of the Bible and vowed to work to end legal abortion.

The political will to use abortion, homosexuality, civil rights for women and other issues of sexual liberation has further bonded the orthodox agenda to the Republican party. This strategy allowed Reagan to unite social conservative voters, largely white, working class and Southern, to the traditional Republican constituency of the economically advantaged. It has since the Reagan administration proved a mixed electoral strategy, as women left the party in significant numbers and gays became a significant politically organized community. For many moderate Republicans, the praising of intolerance as a virtue in the 1992 Republican Platform was a disgrace as well as a mistake. Hence in 1996 a significant pro-choice movement emerged within the party. Bob Dole quickly found that the conservatives would punish any attempt to form a middle ground. For the time Republicans seem locked in an abortion strategy that attracted the orthodox critics of modern tolerance-based morality but repelled a significant pool of American voters.

Ronald Reagan had a natural talent in using punitive social conservatism as a rallying point. He brought a genuineness to drug hate, gay bashing and abortion condemnation that exceeded simple strategic engagement. His campaigns also had a knowledge of how to get different messages to different constituencies, helping him to keep the conservative coalition intact. George Bush actively attempted to profit from these same strategies, with considerably less success.

President Bush devoted his first national address to resurrecting the political magic of Reagan's drug hate, going so far as to stage a dummy bust across the street from the White House for this media event. He stated, "all of us agree that the greatest threat facing our nation is drugs," and proceeded to present for the cameras a bag of crack which he claimed was a sample of drugs routinely sold outside the White House. In fact, agents were ordered to seize a drug courier and get him to the White House, an area of town which as a black kid from the other Washington he proved unable to find on his own. The news media swallowed the theater and followed with an average of four drug stories each day broadcast on each of the national networks for the following month. In this month of drug hate festival, 64 percent of the public came to rank drug use as the nation's worst problem. A year later, as the concerted political and media blitz gave way, this ranking fell to under 10 percent. Except when federally mandated, companies around the nation dropped their drug screening programs, having learned that the detection of drug use in no way predicted job performance.

Also like his predecessor, George Bush discovered that the connection between conservative religion and opposition to abortion rights made for good conservative politics. As one example of this coalition building, he stated to the Catholic Lawyer's Guild, "Use your talent, your energy and your professional resources to ban abortion."[23]

Following this theme in 1991 the Bush Justice Department petitioned in federal court in support of Operation Rescue and their mass attempts to blockade lawful clinics that performed abortions in order to shut them down. The Bush administration blocked the legalization of the abortion drug RU486 and imposed the gag rule precluding federally funded clinics from discussion of abortion. In parallel to the disinformation practices of the government in the War on Drugs, the Bush administration fabricated the claim that aborted fetuses were not useful for medical research. The medical community recognized that this was an expression of ideology posing as medical science. When government exits rational public policy formation and enters angry theology as political focus, the ability to deal with data is lost. In the domestic culture war, as in warfare in general, truth is a victim. Of the ban imposed by the Bush administration, the president of the American Academy of Pediatrics stated, "It's like the Middle Ages. We are very disappointed. The ban interferes with research, with new knowledge that is going to save the lives of fetuses, babies, and adults as well."[24]

President Bush's own vice-president tried hard to use social orthodoxy as the means to create a viable political coalition. Earlier in his career, before President Reagan demonstrated the political use of drug hate, Representative Quayle stated, "Congress should definitely consider decriminalizing possession of marijuana. . . . We should concentrate on the rapists and burglars who are a menace to society."[25] Years later Dan Quayle joined the criminalization drive stating "You want to get on top of a wave while it is cresting."[26] He went on to endorse more funding for the fight against drugs. Later he attempted to use the single-mother character of Murphy Brown to demonstrate his "traditional family values" political credentials.

The political figure who best understood the political uses of the War on Drugs, and the place of drug policy in the overall domestic cultural struggle, was Drug Czar William Bennett. His own career history, as Chairman of the National Endowment for the Humanities (with a mandate to confront and diminish the culture of artists), Secretary of the Department of Education (with a deep and pronounced disdain for the culture of intellect) and finally the greatest Drug Czar, with an understanding that drugs were a metaphor for nonorthodox culture and that drug hate was the key for a culture-cleansing inquisition. In his own book he writes,

> Why is there a battle about our culture? Part of the answer lies in understanding that there is a fundamental difference between many of the most important beliefs of most Americans and the beliefs of a liberal elite that dominate many of our institutions. . . . The elite are most often found among academics and intellectuals, in the literary world, i.e., . . . journals of political opinion, in Hollywood, and in the artistic community, in mainline religious institutions, and in some quarters of the media.[27]

Bennett used his position at the National Endowment for the Humanities to frame in the cultural war the values that would soon take punitive form as the War on Drugs. By 1983 he cut funding to projects that focused on women by more than a third. He cut the number of grants that went to labor unions from 6 the year before he took office to 0. Meanwhile he approved what he called an "emergency grant" to pay for a rhetorical rebuttal to the Public Broadcasting System (PBS) historic series on the Vietnam War.

William Bennett continued the same mission of waging cultural warfare when he was Secretary of Education. Bilingual education, multicultural curriculum and chasing God from the classroom have ruined public education, he submitted. The fundamental lessons should be drawn from the Bible, ancient Greece, European history and the white American experience. He argued for greater use of expulsion from schools to get rid of "rotten kids." Kids caught twice taking any forbidden drugs should be permanently expelled, he urged. Bennett told Congress, "right now, no ifs, ands or buts . . . a clear message to all kids, that if you're using drugs, you're out of school." He submitted that there was no such thing as educating kids into making better choices; only punishment can control behavior. In a departmental publication, *Schools Without Drugs*, he stated, "We have to get tough, and we have to do it now."[28]

When the Supreme Court upheld the First Amendment idea of a separation between church and state as applied to school funding, the future Drug Czar commented that the decision was "crazy, terrible, badly reasoned" and "a ridiculous expression of the court's disdain for religion."[29]

More explicitly than even Ronald Reagan, William Bennett was clear that there were only two kinds of Americans: patriotic loyalists in the War on Drugs and traitors. During his reign the *New Republic* (Oct. 6, 1986) attempted one article designed to foster an understanding of drug use. A reporter actually tried crack and spoke with real users to try to make sense of their lives and choices. The article, entitled "What Crack is Like," reported that "crack is a pleasurable drug with unpleasant side effects," that it can "make sense to demoralized people," and that economic deprivation is responsible for much of the drug's popularity.

The same day that the article was printed, William Bennett described the author as "a defector in the drug war."[30] The nation's Drug Czar submitted that any attempt to understand drug use from the perspective of the user was "garbage." In the ideology of drug hate, understanding is a modern kind of heresy.

Bennett further articulated the patriotic and religious aspect of drug hate in calling for the death penalty for drug dealers. He again compared drug use to treason and so the death penalty "reflects a recognition that the current scourge of drug abuse and of drug-related crime and violence represents a comparable threat to the security and well being of the public, and the use of the ultimate sanction would be available in this context."[31]

In the chapter entitled "The American Nightmare" in his book *The De-valuing of America*, Bennett introduces the stories of a half-dozen fictitious characters and the made-up horror of their lives. He tells for example the story of a 6-month-old child who he claims died of an overdose of crack. No documentation is offered. He further tells of a parent selling her daughter into prostitution to pay for drugs. Bennett argues that the need to promote popular intolerance against drug use places the issue beyond normal truthfulness as a moral consideration. Franklin Zimring and Gordon Hawking, the director and a senior fellow of the Earl Warren Legal Institute at the University of California, concluded of the Drug Czar's published works that there was simply no basis to the data he released regarding drug use. The numbers in his material were simply concocted to achieve manipulation.[32]

Though minorities and the working class are the traditional constituencies of the Democratic party, the most prominent Democrats found joining in the public hate on drugs essential to ride the political waves of the era. Senator Christopher Dodd recognized that "Congress has entered a feeding frenzy."[33] With President Reagan successfully declaring moral war on the issue, Democrats feared that drug hate would prove the popular high ground for the era and spell electoral victory to the most aggressive combatant. They picked up the gauntlet. House Leader Jim Wright stated that his greatest concern was to act before the media lost focus. Democrats accordingly took the President's $1 billion request and multiplied it to $3 billion. Republican Leader of the House Robert Mitchell openly feared that the Democrats were on the verge of running away with the whole issue as Democratic Senator Lloyd Benson accused the Republicans of conducting a "popgun war on Drugs." Of the will in both parties to inflict any punishment so long as it was greeted by public cheer, Congressman Claude Pepper said, "Right now you could put an amendment through to hang, draw and quarter." Congressman Barney Frank quipped, in regard to the piling on of punitive bills, "I'm afraid this is the legislative equivalent of crack. It yields a short-term high but does long-term damage to the system and is expensive to boot."[34]

The pattern for the Democrat's response was set as early as 1982 when Alan Cranston replied for the party to Reagan's kickoff drug war national address. After Reagan announced that he was committing the forces of the nation to domestic war, Cranston stated that it is "refreshing to hear Ronald Reagan suggest that our government can provide a valuable and necessary service to the American people." And so through rhetoric, legislation and spending, congressional Democrats kept the hate wave from politically engulfing them. Bills of the 1986 session included elimination of probation for drug offenses, a new $1 billion for prisons, a new $1 billion for local and state narcotic squads, repeal of the exclusionary rule, and elevation of the Drug Czar to cabinet status. Democratic House Majority leader Jim Wright labeled drugs, "a menace draining away our economy of some $230 billion this year, slowly rotting away the fabric of our society, and seducing and killing our young."[35] No attempt was made to explain how this figure, roughly equal to the whole Social Security budget, was constructed. The modern drug war during the Reagan-Bush administrations cost the tax payer in excess of $150 billion. That sort of waste requires bipartisan cooperation.

Bill Clinton wrested the White House from 12 years of Republican rule. He did so in part by adopting much of the Reagan Revolution agenda to form what he called "New Democrats." Some would suggest that Bill Clinton was to Ronald Reagan as Dwight Eisenhower was to Franklin Roosevelt. Eisenhower led the Republicans back to the White House, but only by accepting the fundamental economic liberal agenda that included social security and protection of labor unions. Under the Clinton administration prisons continued their rise in construction and black teenagers continued to fill them in large numbers. Yet, as Eisenhower by personality and direction of interest moved the country away from waging domestic class conflict, so too Clinton has lowered the demand for cultural warfare, and so drugs entered a period of institutionalized police and prison stability rather than centrality in political engagement.

When the drug war was young, hot and focal, other actors beside politicians found it useful and potent. Consideration of the other beneficiaries and contributors to this dark domestic movement is the subject of the rest of this chapter. In 1986, *Time* and *Newsweek* each ran 5 cover stories on drugs. The three networks broadcast 74 segments on drugs in just the month of July in 1989. Titles of such programs included "Drugs: One Nation Under Siege," by CBS (Central Broadcasting System) and "Drugs: A Plague on America" by NBC (National Broadcasting Corporation). During the era of the savings and loan scandal and the creation of the federal debt, the media knew well that drugs made much better theater and gave this issue so much attention as to preclude coverage of less sensational but more substantive news. Before a further examination of the use of drugs-as-theater for news media, let us consider other participants in the media's portion of the drug hate phenomena.

Advertising formed a different front. In 1987 the Partnership for a Drug-Free America was established as an effort by advertizing firms to enter the cause. They introduced a whole array of passion-arousing presentations to the public's drug consciousness. Images include a surgeon clumsily cutting into an unanesthetized patient with a scalpel while laughing weirdly and puffing on a marijuana cigarette. The announcer then asks, "Who says drugs have no victims?" Such manipulations add nothing to the dialogue, but they successfully rouse popular hate. Paid advertized drug hate commercials became an art form, a chance for advertisers to practice the craft of manipulation without any concern with honesty. Images such as 2 charred eggs referred to as "your brain on drugs" became nationally recognizable. If such baseless theater had been used in the advertizing of products, The Federal Trade Commission's and Federal Communication Commission's rules on honesty would have come into play. Drugs provided a unique opportunity for manipulation without rules or moral restraint.

Entertainment television has also substantially accepted the mandate to help foster public intolerance. NBC's vice-president for programming standards and community relations declared that every drug-using character must suffer and that the network is "returning scripts where we very specifically say this particular character must suffer more in the end." Johnathan Estrin, writer of "Cagney and Lacey," said, "We have again fallen prey to the hot issue of the moment. It's such an easy target. . . . And the loyalty oath atmosphere, the me-tooism, makes me a little uncomfortable."[36]

The movies enjoyed the hate and used it as the new context for entertaining graphic violence. Characters from local cops to James Bond were allowed to beat drug dealers without legal restraint. Thus drugs took on a role formerly assigned to Soviet operatives and international terrorists. The use of drugs as simply filling the human want for a socially legitimate focus for hate will be further considered in this chapter.

Middle American anti-intellectual journals led the drug hate trend in the print media. In particular *Reader's Digest*, *Saturday Evening Post* and *Ladies' Home Journal* all discovered that their clientele had a pent-up rage against cultural change that translated into an appetite for drug hate stories. Millions of people read week after week that drugs were the threat to parental authority and the reason Mom and Dad could not raise the kids right. These publications selected and fabricated studies on marijuana to make claims that drugs led to sexual promiscuity, heart attack, cancer, sterility and big breasts on boys. *Reader's Digest* in particular sold 3 million reprints of the article in which they claimed that teenage culture is drug laden and driven by rock music to rebel against parental authority. Parents were informed quite clearly that all the faults of the offspring were not the consequence of poor parenting. Rather, a permissive culture wrapped around drug use and 1960s motifs was the cause of teenage disobedience and failure, and so it was the appropriate focus for blame. The late baby-boomers were about to be punished for the liberation behavior of their older brothers and sisters.

Yet the most infamous drug hate abuse by the media is held by one of the jewels of elite journalism, the *Washington Post*. On September 28, 1980, the newspaper ran on page 1 a story of "Jimmy," a black 8-year-old who for the past three years was a heroin addict. The article described the needle sliding into his arm as his mother watched her live-in lover administer a dose "sending the fourth grader into a hypnotic nod."

Mayor Marion Barry launched a city-wide search to find Jimmy. Teachers were ordered to inspect the arms of every boy in the city. A $10,000 reward was offered for information on the boy. Neither Jimmy nor any other child addict was ever found.

Six months later the *Post* nominated the article for a Pulitzer Prize. Bob Woodward, assistant managing editor, had already expressed doubt of the authenticity of the piece, but felt that without a retraction he could not avoid the nomination of so sensational a story. The Pulitzer committee gave the article the nation's highest journalism award. Right after, the author confessed to making the whole thing up. Though it lacked all factual authenticity, the article struck the fancy of an era ready for the drug hate. No one asked, is it likely that addicts who steal for their daily dose would share so freely an expensive drug, or that a child would so willingly accept a needle to the arm? The lesson learned by journalism at large was how well drug hate sells and how little actual research need go into a good drug hate story to be a market success. Elite news journalism joined the tabloids, advertising forums, and programming in realizing that there was a public taste for drug hate pieces, and they sought to cater to that taste as part of the business side of journalism.

Newsweek learned the lesson. "Joint by joint, line by line, pill by pill," the magazine reported "the use of illegal drugs on the job has become a crisis for American business . . . Some experts even suggest that one reason the United States is losing its industrial leadership to Japan is that America's work force is stoned."[37] *U.S. News and World Report* could not let a competitor run away with the emotionally fashionable, even if factually vacuous, story of the era, so they reported in 1993 that drug use was "so widespread among adults that it threatens to sap the nation's strength at a critical juncture in history. . . . No one has measured how all this pill popping, injecting and inhaling has effected the national output. Yet the growth of US productivity has been lagging behind that of other major industrial nations, none of which has a drug problem as serious." When the U.S. economy proved the strongest in the developed world in the 1990s, during a period of increasing drug use, there were no retractions of this assertion that the pleasure sins of the workers were the root cause of decline. Similarly poor management decisions and lavish return to executives and capital were also not considered. Well-paid reporters and publishers kept the blame focused on life-style decisions of the workers.

Subjugation of the working class thus forms a partial explanation of the use of drug hate. Racial subjugation is a more important use. Media use of the rise of crack in the 1980s highlights this. Alcohol and tobacco are the number 1 and number 2 causes for fetal low birth weight. But the white demographics of these drugs always have limited the moral use of these sins. Then in 1985 a media feeding frenzy erupted as it was decided that crack produced low birth weight among primarily blacks. The study on which this conclusion was based considered 23 women who used crack and had miscarriages or potentially harmed babies. All of these women also drank alcohol and smoked cigarettes, but there was no interest in reporting that. So the media concocted a disease of "crack babies," and every network showed footage of small babies screaming in withdrawal. Claire Cole at Emory University Medical School discovered that the networks were actually filming babies in withdrawal from heroin and calling it crack. Babies subjected to real crack and cocaine do not scream; they sleep as the effects of the stimulant expire.

CBS reported that "crack babies" would never achieve an IQ above 50, and would be barely able to dress themselves and live alone. Subsequent study shows the contrary. These babies grow up and ten years later perform normally for social and economic conditions. *Newsweek* again had it right for marketing purposes. The Jan. 24, 1983 issue that ran an article about a teenager snorting coke in his suburban home sold 15 percent more than average. Recognizing a good thing, the editors devoted another issue to crack and said, "an epidemic is abroad in America as pervasive and dangerous in its way as the plagues of medieval times." That year fewer than 600 Americans died from cocaine and crack; the plagues killed a third of Europe. All of this media drug hate helped fuel demand for mass punishment, rather than a willingness to fund public health programs.

Television reached its high point in exploitation of drug hate in 1986 with the introduction of live-raid footage, introducing the ability to have staged theater of warfare in peace time with real bullets for extra dramatic flourish. ABC (American Broadcasting Corporation) introduced this style of made-for-TV action-packed news as the network coordinated with the DEA to smash with battering rams into a house. A modern form of cinema swept the electronic media, as one official put it, this "is the hottest combat-reporting story to come along since the end of the Vietnam War."[38] Police in ski masks smashing down residential doors became synonymous with the "good-guy" as the new real action hero.

The networks knew they had a good thing, dramatic footage that appealed to the nation's entertainment tastes and came from the government at no cost. Fifteen million people watched CBS news run a docu-drama called "48 hours on Crack Street." Four days later NBC replied with "Cocaine Country." Geraldo Rivera topped them all with the "The Doping of a Nation," a solid hour of gun fire and battering rams cut from nothing but raid footage and other thrilling scenes. *Newsweek* and *Time* tried to keep up by making drugs their cover story five times each in 1986.

As it became clear that the American people had an insatiable appetite for cop raids, television further blurred the gap between drama and news with shows such as "Cops" on the Fox network and "Top Cops" on CBS. These shows proved both popular and cheap. Local police departments were delighted for the chance to see themselves highlighted weekly and were willing to donate the staff and equipment to make the shoot cheap. The director of "Top Cops" explained that the theme of the program was to help the viewer to witness the evil of the individual criminal against the backdrop of a benign police force so the public will see police operations as legitimate and worth support.[39] He acknowledged a purposeful attempt to never consider drug taking and crime as aspects of complex social failures and pressures.

It is fair to say that the behavior of the media is one of the significant portions of the intensity of the public hate surrounding drugs. Jimmie Reeves and Richard Campbell attempt to explain the abandonment of the press in any interest in truth or investigation on this issue in their book *Cracked Coverage: Television News, The Anti-Cocaine Crusade, and the Reagan Legacy*. All three networks refused to allow still pictures from their docu-dramas to be included in this book. Perhaps the networks are rightfully embarrassed in the way they exploited the destructive forces of this decade of drug hate to increase their own market share.

The author's thesis is that "the journalistic recruitment in the anti-cocaine crusade was absolutely crucial to converting the war on drugs into a political spectacle that depicted social problems grounded on economic transformation as individual moral or behavioral problems that could be remedied by simply embracing family values, policing mean streets, and incarcerating all the fiendish enemies within." They trace the movement of television coverage of cocaine from under 60 stories per year on all three networks to 150 per year during wartime coverage in 1985–1986 as blacks were targeted for their use of cheap adulterated cocaine labeled crack. Earlier, when cocaine was a middle-class white drug, therapy was the prescribed remedy to end addiction; once crack became prevalent, prison was the prescribed remedy.

As media became devoted to covering this made-up war, it came to rely on persons who made their living off the war as experts. Thus police and drug therapists gave one side of a story, telling of the need for public funds to help them fight and win this domestic war, and no journalistic source saw itself as a neutral truth finder. Neutrality made bad business sense and violated an idea that this was an issue in which media could repent from its critical coverage during Watergate and Vietnam and join the "morning in America" age. Critics of the drug policy were accordingly not included in public debate until the 1990s. Drug war professionals thus for a time both controlled the presentation and profited from the resulting policies. Networks and their experts achieved a steady state of crises for years that gave the networks valuable stories that were highly popular and easy to produce. The age of the investigative reporter, focal during the Vietnam War and Watergate, was replaced by government propagandist as alley in the War on Drugs. Media found cooperation with those in power easier, more popular and far more profitable than exploration for truths.

Government cooperated by continuously producing media events on drugs that justified the focus away from more real and embarrassing public policy issues such as declining wages, rising homelessness and Social Security insolvency. Other events, such as the deaths of actors and sports figures were fit in to continue the crisis coverage and to legitimate the drug war as the story of the decade.

Focus on drugs becomes a means of reinforcing a whole moral-political-economic hierarchy of society and made the media essentially conservative in a conservative era. Loser groups in our society were further victimized as winner groups were reinforced in their higher status. Experts, politicians, media giants, and the upper economic class all win as workers, the poor, minorities and sinners all loose. The War on Drugs reinforced through media authority a conservative hierarchical society backed up by increased bureaucratic and police power given legitimacy through the created drug crises.

A focal media manipulation was the discrepancy in coverage between the treatment of white cocaine offenders and crack-using black delinquents. Between 1981 and 1985, when cocaine was defined as a recreational drug for the prosperous white, the coverage was framed by a medical model in which the offender can be helped once the offending behavior is recognized and denounced. The moral of telling the story of the drug user is as a cautionary tale to others who might consider abandoning the limits of conforming middle-class behavior. The role of media is to uphold orthodox normal behavior against the assault of forbidden choices made possible in this post-1960s' bad "new age." This is in stark contrast to the siege paradigm regulating the crisis coverage starting in 1986, when cocaine came to be seen as urban, black and poor. Then only massive punishment or a full-scale war against the domestic enemy could save the nation. The user was no longer treatable under a medical model; instead he must be incarcerated to save larger society.

The media's job then was to raise the alarm of the enemy within.

In the crisis phase of reporting, journalism joins government in explaining that the drug is pure evil. Stories are released of children killing parents for drug money, and the media under the new paradigm of journalism as government propagandist tells the story rather than investigating its authenticity. Into this made-for-popular-drama came the setting of den of iniquity, the crack house, the perfect "locus of evil" for a culture war in which white conservative America re-takes control at gun point after a decade of stumbling and doubt. The television crew is sent in to show the story only from the perspective of the invading police assaulting a foreign enemy. No attempt is ever made to see the war from the perspective of the victims. The media never humanizes the enemy as it had in Vietnam.

By 1988 half the total drug stories on network television were staged dramatic armed raids on city crack houses. The most famous raid occurred on April 6, 1989, when LAPD chief Daryl Gates and Nancy Reagan sat in a luxury motor home labeled "The Establishment," eating fruit salad. Across the street a SWAT team surrounded a crack house. Nancy Reagan fixed her make-up while the swat team bound the helpless black teenagers. She emerged sporting a LAPD windbreaker to declare, "These people in here are beyond the point of teaching and rehabilitation." They were carted off as proof that the enemies of normal America have had their day and now shall be crushed.

The authors submit that "in the amphetamine-like journalistic frenzy of the summer of 1986, many reporters became gung-ho recruits in the war on drugs who, consciously or unconsciously, also championed both the nostalgia and the backlash politics of the New Right."[40] The War on Drugs gave the media a profitable and highly visual means of endorsing the right-wing view that punishment of urban minority sin was the focal domestic agenda. In a 40-week period the nation's four major newspapers and three top weekly news magazines kicked out 406 drug stories. The *New York Times* led with 139 stories. Public interest in the issue recorded a parallel jump, moving from 2 percent identifying drugs as the most significant national problem to 80 percent, after the media blitz, agreeing that the nation was caught up in a major drug crisis. Fascinatingly, even at the height of the drug scare, 62 percent of the public recognized that in opposition to the barrage of media stories, drugs were not a significant problem in their own towns. People knew people who recreationally took drugs, mostly marijuana, but could not think of a person they would describe as harmed by consumption of illegal drugs. The public looked for an enemy they were warned against by the government and media and concluded it must exist somewhere else. As during McCarthyism, everyone believed there to be a vast communist conspiracy in theory; they just did not happen to personally know any drug users who were a public menace.

For the media, drugs presented an opportunity to move into wartime journalism during a time of peace. Daily footage of uniformed warriors smashing domestic evil was both profitable and exciting. This was not primarily an ideological endorsement of Reaganism; it was a business opportunity for the enterprise as a whole and a career opportunity for individual reporters to cast off their professional truth-seeking norms and saddle up with the cavalry for a safe but exciting adventure in the urban wilds. Thus one supporting leg to this politician-led domestic crusade has become clear.

For America's orthodox religions the assault on alternative culture was more heart-felt and genuine. During the era of the War on Drugs, the religious right launched a broad offensive against new culture. During this conservative era the many orthodox churches of the nation were united by a sense of confrontation with new culture that had emerged since the 1960s. Catholic, evangelic and fundamentalist Protestants, Mormons and Orthodox Jews found common cause in denunciation of pornography, homosexuality, abortion, the right to die, feminism, the Internet, public education and Hollywood. Martin Marty, editor of the *Fundamentalist Project*, explains that this American revival of orthodoxy was a portion of a worldwide phenomena. Traditionalist religions around the world found the mass pleasure-seeking secular liberal culture a threat. Orthodox religions retaliated to turn back the clock to an age, possibly fictitious, in which their values, norms and scriptures were central. In America, as drugs had been a part of the cultural force that challenged the 1950s in the 1960s and 1970s, they were a target of those who sought to undo the liberal order in the conservative revolution of the 1980s and 1990s.

Fundamentalists turned to television on a massive scale. By 1985 the top 20 religious programs had 11 million regular viewers. Most of these programs spent much of the day condemning modern culture. The counter-culture and its associated drug use were particular targets. Pat Robertson, Jerry Falwell and the Pope joined in firm agreement that modern society had granted too many rights to the individual in disregard to the moral limits imposed by traditional religious culture. Falwell labeled the election of 1980 as "the greatest day for the cause of conservatism in my adult life."[41] Pat Robertson would attempt to continue this momentum into the 1990s with the Christian Coalition. The Southern Baptist Church, largest and most politically active of the Protestant denominations, by 1997 began a boycott against the Disney Corporation for their corrupting cultural influence. Their membership felt under assault from an array of sources, including programing that most of the nation saw as sweet, wholesome and very normal. If Disney was a threat, the existence of MTV and "60 Minutes" must have been shocking. In studying their views sociologist Nancy Ammerman writes, "we're finding that the fundamentalists are madder, they're more discontented, more alienated and by virtue of that discontent have a lot more momentum behind their efforts at the political convention."[42]

As previously noted, the inclusion of orthodox belief in the Republican circle both created the Republican majority and changed the party's identity. By 1984 the fundamentalist Protestant vote split 81-to-19 in favor of Republicans, a considerable shift from the 56-to-44 split favoring the Democrats in 1976. The central rallying cry of this conversion was that the sins of modern society must be swept away through law and punishment.

A strong parallel is thus made to the nation's earlier experience in mass criminalization of the intoxicated during Prohibition. Rural white Protestant fundamentalists were the driving force behind the attempt to criminalize urban immigrant Catholics and so regain cultural hegemony. By the 1980s orthodox Catholics and Protestants had joined forces with other like-minded churches to criminalize the urban blacks and cultural rebels. In the contemporary drug war the two most important correlates to states that embraced the criminalization agenda were found to be the growth of a minority ethnic population and large membership in orthodox religion. In particular the author of *The Politics of Sin*, a study on the causes of popularity of drug punishment, found that "church membership is correlated with criminalization of marijuana and large fines for violations."[43] Churches have an impact in promoting criminalization but no impact in promoting abstinence. High membership in organized traditional religion breeds an intolerance to behavior defined as sinful, but does not correlate to abstinence of those defined sins.

The importance of fundamentalist religion in the Bible Belt of the Southeast and Midwest helps to explain the particular desire for criminalization of blacks for drug sin. Religious denunciation became a sanitized means of traditional racial oppression. Orthodox religion promised a return to the "good old days" which in America has strong racial implications. And so the crack house and crack mother served as reference to the long tradition of seeing blacks as foreign, evil and corrupting. Thus another aspect to the success of the drug war as essential policy of the nation for an era is added. Orthodox religions join politicians and the media as supporters of the War on Drugs. The predominance of white Southern and rural demographics in the orthodox cause helps to introduce race as the next element.

Overall drug use by blacks and other minorities differs little from whites. The will to intoxication is a human constant in which no ethnic group is particularly represented or absent. But drug laws became an accepted and politically desired means for the majority to target minorities with criminal punishment. The racial aspect of the criminalization of other people's drug use is true throughout the century of attempted drug prohibition. Opiates were criminalized in the early 1910s as a means of dealing with the growing Oriental population. Alcohol criminalization was a way of rural Protestant whites to check the growing urban Catholic population. Marijuana became criminal after a long history of agricultural use when "undesired" Mexican and black populations became associated with the drug. The banning of marijuana in the West parallels the rise of anti-Mexican sentiment in the 1910s and 1920s.[44] Every demographic group has its culturally defined form of intoxication. Criminalization of other groups' selections is a way of legitimating and enacting chauvinism as the police administer the desired oppression in the name of justice.

The basic laws that exist today testify to this race aspect. Real cocaine is punished for 500 grams at the rate of 5 grams of crack. Ninety-seven percent of persons criminalized by the crack laws are black. Not coincidently, a survey of persons who voted Democratic for economic reasons then moved to the Republican party in the 1980s show a strong distaste for blacks. The quality of life was measured in this group by distance from blacks: "not being black is what constituted being middle class, not living with blacks is what made a neighborhood a decent place to live."[45] Drug criminalization became the way to appeal to racial intolerance while wearing the righteous robes of opposition to sin rather than the racist Ku Klux Klan garb. Jesse Helms of North Carolina in 1988 introduced the bill to create a mandatory minimum for the possession of the crack form of cocaine. Five years for 5 grams with no chance of parole. By 1997 1-in-7 black males were barred from voting by reason of a felony conviction. Between 1986 and 1991 incarceration of black males for drug violations increased 465 percent.[46] Between 1985 and 1987 99 percent of drug-trafficking defendants nationwide were black. By 1997 a third of all black males under the age of 30 were under the control of the criminal justice system. Race is a powerful aspect of explaining the popularity of a public policy that called for the nation to declare war against selected portions of itself.

Class conflict also must be considered as a portion of the explanation of why drug hate dominated public policy. In the prior liberal era, the Great Society policy platform suggested that poverty had social causes and relief from poverty was society's responsibility. These welfare wealth redistribution programs were from the start a target of the conservative movement and the Reagan administration. Drug hate allowed a fundamental philosophical shift in the understanding of poverty. To replace the notion that poverty was a social problem, curable through public health, public housing, public jobs, and other programs, the new paradigm instructed that poverty was a moral failure on the part of the impoverished individual. This is a shift from viewing the downtrodden as people in trouble who deserve to be helped in the name of basic humanitarian or religious moral principles to seeing them as people who cause trouble and so deserve to be punished or eliminated to make way for the more worthy. Again William Bennett most explicitly stated the case for the great shift in paradigms from government as social helper to mass economic punisher. As Drug Czar, he wrote in the 1989 *National Drug Control Strategy*, "We must avoid the easy temptation to blame our troubles first on those chronic problems of social environment—like poverty and racism—which help to breed and spread the contagion of drug use."

During the conservative era, the basic humanitarian relief programs in the United States were reduced and eliminated. The jobs and housing programs were even more definitively targeted and destroyed. But the rising importance of police as the essential domestic policy helped to offset the inherent social dangers of a growing underclass.

The popularity and centrality of the drug war has been explained as a benefit to successful drug warrior politicians, a source of profit for use by the media, an extension of a religious orthodox ethic that forbidden pleasures must be punished in order to achieve restoration of the past, an instrument of racial antagonism and as a means to undo the liberal consensus to aid the poor through policy package of welfare. The War on Drugs is finally an affirmation of the prime conservative values of hierarchy and obedience: citizen to state, child to parent, public to police, employee to employer, sinner to minister, deviant individual to dominant culture. Again Bennett articulates the fundamental point in an address before the Conservative Washington Hebrew Congregation: "The drug crisis is a crisis of authority in every sense of the term, 'authority.' "[47]

Most fundamentally the War on Drugs was a means of attacking that portion of American culture that decided that the meaning of freedom as promised in the nation's fundamental text was the right to make personal choices. William Bennett, as always, is blunt in stating the cause of the drug conflict: it "comes from the tradition of freedom and liberty which gets distorted into license and 'do your own thing' and the gospel of the sixties."[48]

The most potent of the forms of reassertion of traditional authority relations that the drug war facilitated is intergenerational, parents over children, tradition over new ways. In the liberal era youth proved that the parent generation was wrong about many things: the reliability of government, the usefulness of orthodox tradition to life in the modern world, the war in Vietnam, the harmfulness of pot, and so on. The drug war in many ways was pay-back time and a reassertion of the conservative view that those in power do not need to prove their point; they can simply punish non-conforming articulations into submission. It is precisely the unique cultural and physical aspects of marijuana that made the War on Drugs the focus of public policy. Marijuana was the cultural icon of rebellious youth. At the end of the Carter era 1 in 9 high-school seniors smoked pot daily. Sixteen years later half of high-school seniors still light up at some time during the year. The absence of physical harm from smoking pot has required that all the punitive force be government created. Punishment for marijuana is thus the great frontier of authoritarianism. A widespread popular behavior detested by the ruling culture has justified war propaganda, police engagement and mass punishment. A new movement began which counseled parents to quit trying to be understanding friends to their kids and develop a *toughlove* capacity to squelch all individuality and nonconformity in the name of drug resistance. Music selection, clothes choices, hair length all were appropriate instruments for parents to prove that they had rightful plenary power. The Reagan administration produced *Parent Peers & Pot* to encourage parents to view every expression of independence as an embrace of drug culture. The Zeitgeist of siding with youth and liberation in the 1960s was replaced with "Just Say No" as a way of creating hierarchical rule. The basic cultural tide had shifted from liberation embracing to control embracing.

Toughlove,[49] as both a book and a movement encouraged parents to squelch all elements of independence among their offspring. Any disobedience should be seen as a prelude to drug abuse and family revolution and met with banishment. Straight Inc. took this notion one step further and provided a check-in prison system for parents to deposit their kids. At its zenith this private enterprise established centers in 14 states. The owners of these for-profit prisons insulated themselves from criminal indictment by repeating the rhetoric of the drug war era and by campaign donations to the most prominent drug hate politicians. Court papers, once investigation finally occurred, showed routine beatings, sleep and food deprivation and squalid conditions.

For some portion of Americans drug hate takes on a personally meaningful moral patriotism that must be considered as a sociological event. Psychologists Terry Bulych and Barry Beyerstein consider the pathology of drug war enthusiasts. They find a high need for dogmatism among persons anxious for drug punishment. They want an ordered world of firm right and wrong in which sin is punished for denunciation value. As a personality type, drug war enthusiasts are the people who would have enthusiastically joined in the brooding hunt for deviance during the McCarthy era. These people turn to the War on Drugs to fill a void lost by the end of the cold war. Bulych and Beyerstein conclude that,

> respondents who favored the drug war were particularly apt to construe as factually correct the highly sensationalized cinematic portrayal of the drug scene. With the decline of the worldwide Communist threat that was formerly used to justify gratuitous violence in the movies, the industry has turned, with considerable audience approval, to the drug dealer stereotype when in need of an acceptable villain to dismember in living color.[50]

Ronald Reagan, as a man who entered public affairs as an activist rooting out communist influences in Hollywood, became a natural leader of this will to transform other people's drug use into a personally meaningful crusade among moralists unhappy with social transformation.

There has been much psychological study of the "addictive personality." In the end that has not proven a fruitful topic, as all cultures at all times are revealed to engage in intoxication which turns out to be a common factor of the human equation.[51] Once alcohol, nicotine and caffeine are added as genuine drugs most Americans turn out to be users. Of far more importance is exploration of the essential psychology of the drug war enthusiast. It is comparatively easy to understand why people take drugs as a means of pleasure seeking, an anesthetic against pain and for reasons of community formation, rebellion, revelation and self-exploration. It is comparatively hard to understand why hatred of other people's forbidden acts becomes an obsession of so many. The punishment-craving personality must be added as explanation for this age of celebrated punitive excess.

The political alignment that drove the War on Drugs during the Reagan-Bush era has declined in its clear hegemony over the nation's politics. It is less clear in the late 1990s that punitive cultural conservatism is the magic political formula that Nixon articulated, Reagan formed and Bush struggled to mount. The meaning of shifting political potentials as the nation moves away from drug hate as the hub of political order is the topic of the next chapter. Now it is important to ask the question, why if the hard political demand for a War on Drugs based on conservative, racist, classist, psychological and religious moral values is no longer politically triumphant, does the mass incarceration continue? A portion of the answer is the lack of a Franklin D. Roosevelt–like figure wise enough to re-end Prohibition. A different answer is that bureaucratic and institutional forces that prospered from the war refuse to allow peace and thus work hard to maintain war spending, measured from total state, local and federal sources at $70 billion in 1996. This figure is still rising.[52]

For the whole 80 years of national drug prohibition, bureaucratic attempts to sell punitive abundance to the public joined racism, psychological love of punishment, puritanism and cultural chauvinism as factors in the policy arena. In the prohibition of marijuana, the absence of personal or social harm from the drug has necessitated high levels of administratively generated drug hate propaganda. The "Reefer Madness" era lacks some of the sophistication of modern propaganda but captures many of the same elements still deployed.

A significant power of bureaucratic agencies is to use the legitimacy of office to lend credibility to disinformation designed to produce useful public hate. William Bennett is the significant modern practitioner, before him came J. Edgar Hoover and his service to the demonization of alcohol and Harry Anslinger, who most successfully of all fostered a culture of drug hate and used it to build a permanent niche in the federal government for the Federal Bureau of Narcotics. By the mid-1930s Anslinger had mastered the technique of fabricating anecdotal stories of rape, murder, mayhem and madness tied to marijuana, and presenting these as proof of the important work of his agency. "Reefer Madness" is the most famous of the many articles and stories produced or sponsored by the agency. The movie *Reefer Madness*, in fact, differs little from contemporary "crack baby" and "Jimmy" stories. Also then, as today, the agency actively worked to suppress the scientific data that routinely contradicted the bureaucratic claim of drug harm. One such instance is when the Russell Sage Foundation was threatened in the 1950s with loss of their tax-exempt status for offering to publish the joint American Bar Association (ABA)–American Medical Association (AMA) report showing that drug criminalization was ineffective and harmful.

A parallel manipulation by the contemporary bureaucracy is offered by DARE. This police agency, originally founded by the LAPD, receives $600 million in tax payer money and is taught in 70 percent of the nation's schools. After years of successfully avoiding review of the DARE program, the Research Triangle Institute was hired to review the impact deployment of police officers in the nation's schools had. Not surprisingly evaluation determined that sending police into schools to scare the kids turned out to be ineffective. During the period of high use of the DARE program, use of drugs by high-school students has returned to being a normal majority experience. DARE only repeats the most blatantly propagandistic drug hate disinformation, and so even the youngest students are quickly able to perceive they are being lied to.

New Republic magazine broke the story of the lengths DARE went to in an effort to suppress this data. The article disclosed that "What studies have shown is that the program doesn't work. And those who say so have been shut down. America's top drug prevention program doesn't work. But you had better not say so."[53] DARE flooded the Justice Department, who initially sponsored the study through a subsidiary called the Justice Institute, to suppress publication of the results. DARE also lobbied Congress and in 1994 the Justice Department agreed to suppress the findings. When the *American Journal of Public Health* [87(10): Oct. 1997] finally published the story, after validating its methodology and results through a peer review process, DARE turned its fire on them. When the journal published the article, it ran a statement from the editor: "DARE has tried to interfere with the publication of this. They tried to intimidate us."

In the modern era an array of bureaucratic agencies require significant levels of drug hate to sustain their own existence. Unlike other agencies, there is no beneficiary group among the public dependent on drug persecution. This causes agencies to be particularly anxious to create the public anger necessary to maintain their accustomed prime funding levels.

Phantom numbers are one means the bureaucracy utilizes to maintain its funding. Numbers play an important role in drug funding. The public must continuously believe that drugs are prevalent and dangerous and that the problem would be worse except for the excellent job done by the drug agencies and that a reduction in funding would increase use, crime and violence. Thus New York City released numbers regarding thefts attributed to the city's heroine users. An article in the journal *The Public Interest* showed these numbers to exceed 1,200 percent of all reported theft.[54] Most of drug policy involves issues difficult to measure and open to values in presentation. If 15% of high-school-aged marijuana smokers at some time go on to snort cocaine, as the Michigan survey suggests, then 85% do not. It is a matter of conjecture then whether marijuana is a gateway drug. The bureaucracy is there to ensure that all numbers are interpreted in a manner friendly to the sustained war effort.

As drug war victims became the majority of federal prisoners and the biggest category of state prisoners, the prison guard unions joined federal and state police departments as drug war supporters. The number of corrections officers more than doubled during the Reagan-Bush era, a period in which most public hiring was flat. It is no surprise that one of the correlates of stronger drug criminalization legislation is larger police employment lobbying for labor consuming punitive laws.[55] In 1991 The National Conference on Crime changed its name to the National Conference on Crime and Drugs to reflect that when the nation's local police chief gather "all we do is meet about the drug problem" in the word of the Washington, D.C. Chief of Police. Drugs as an issue increased the power of police departments, and as they became more powerful, they proved more fully able to protect their niche. Laws allowing police to keep forfeit assets add incentive to stay away from violent crime and concentrate on drug sin. The Justice Department seized $1.5 billion in the years 1986–1990. In 1991 80 percent of the people who had their property taken never were even charged with a crime. Police were satisfied to simply have the assets. All of this helps to maintain the post–War on Drugs punitive status quo.

NOTES

1. "Crackdown on Drugs Brings Fear to Border," *New York Times*, Dec. 26, 1996.
2. "Ghost Town That Was Restored to Life is Now in Uproar Over Raid for Drugs," *New York Times*, March 9, 1985.
3. "City Seeks to Dislodge Drug Trade by Demolishing Tenement Havens," *New York Times*, July 18, 1982.
4. "Federal Agents Cut Drug Traffic," *New York Times*, May 2, 1982.
5. "Washington Finds Drug War is Hardest at Home," *New York Times*, Dec. 9, 1988.
6. Dan Baum, *Smoke and Mirrors*, Boston, Little Brown and Co., 236.

7. "Dispute on Religion Raised by Campaign," *New York Times*, Nov. 9, 1980.

8. "Reverend Reagan," *New Republic* (April 4, 1983).

9. David Sadofsky, *The Question of Privacy in Public Policy* (Westport, CT, Praeger, 1993), p. 86.

10. "Ueberroth Orders Wide Tests for Drug Use in Pro Baseball," *New York Times*, May 8, 1985.

11. "Reagan in Radio Talk, Vows Drive Against Drugs," *New York Times*, Oct. 3, 1982.

12. "Reagan Advocates Crusade on Drugs," *New York Times*, Sept. 15, 1986.

13. "Text of President's Speech on Drive Against Crime," *New York Times*, Oct. 15, 1982.

14. "Reagan Plans Bigger Budget for U.S. Law Enforcement," *New York Times*, Jan. 2, 1984.

15. Dan Baum, *Smoke and Mirrors*, p. 171

16. "Nancy Reagan: How Parents Can Help Teenage Drug Users," *U.S. News & World Report*, May 31, 1982.

17. "Meese in a Move on Pornography, Creates Special Prosecution Team," *New York Times*, Oct. 23, 1986.

18. "Playboy and Book Sellers Suing Pornography Panel," *New York Times*, May 20, 1986.

19. Ibid.

20. "Report Draws Strong Praise and Criticism," *New York Times*, July 10, 1986.

21. "Meese, in a Move on Pornography Creates Special Prosecution Team," *New York Times*, Oct. 23, 1986.

22. "President Denounces Abortion as Murder," *New York Times*, June 24, 1986.

23. "Bush Asks Action Against Abortion," *New York Times*, Sept. 24, 1989.

24. "Citing Abortion, U.S. Extends Ban of Grants for Fetal Tissue Work," *New York Times*, Nov. 2, 1989.

25. Dan Baum, *Smoke and Mirrors*, p. 92

26. Ibid.

27. William Bennett, *The De-valuing of America* (New York, Summit Books, 1992), 18.

28. Ibid.

29. "Bennett Assails Justices on Disdain for Religion," *New York Times*, July 3, 1985.

30. David Sadofsky, *The Question of Privacy in Public Policy* (Westport, CT: Praeger, 1993), 139.

31. "Administration Offers Tough New Drug Bill," *New York Times*, May 17, 1990.

32. Franklin Zimring, *Prison Population and Criminal Justice Policy in California* (Berkeley, University of California Press, 1992).

33. "In 1988 Election Drug Issue #1 in People's Mind," *New York Times*, May 22, 1988.

34. "House Approves U.S. Military to Fight Drugs," *New York Times*, Sept. 12, 1986.

35. Dan Baum, *Smoke and Mirrors*, p. 231

36. "Nancy Reagan Urges TV Roles that Reject Drugs," *New York Times*, Nov. 1, 1986.

37. Dan Baum, *Smoke and Mirrors*, p. 187.

38. Ibid., p. 226.

39. Jimmie Reeves and Richard Campbell, *Cracked Coverage* (Durham, Duke University Press, 1994), 256.

40. Ibid., p. 150.

41. "Dispute on Religion Raised by Campaign," *New York Times*, May 17, 1980.

42. "More Than Bible Is at Issue as Southern Baptists Gather," *New York Times*, June 6, 1986.

43. Kenneth Meier, *The Politics of Sin* (Armonk, NY, M. E. Sharp, 1994), p. 110.

44. Ibid., p. 33.

45. Dan Baum, *Smoke and Mirrors*, p. 223.

46. *Drug Policy Letter*, Number 28, Winter 1996, p. 10.

47. *Drug Policy Letter*, Number 32, Winter/Spring 1997.

48. Dan Baum, *Smoke and Mirrors*, p. 291.

49. Phyllis York and Ted Wetchel, *Toughlove* (New York, Doubleday, 1982).

50. Terry Bulych and Barry Beyerstein, "Authoritarianism and Misinformation as Sources of Support for the War on Drugs," in *New Frontiers in Drug Policy* (Washington, D.C., The Drug Policy Foundation, 1991).

51. Ronald Siegel, *Intoxication* (New York, E. P. Dutton, 1989).

52. *National Review*, Feb. 12, 1996, p. 34.

53. "Don't You Dare," *New Republic*, March 3, 1997.

54. "The Vitality of Mythical Number," Max Singer, *The Public Interest*, Issue 23, 1971, p. 3.

55. Kenneth Meier, *The Politics of Sin*, p. 112.

6

The Passing of the Hate Age?

Can society save itself from the ravages of drug hate? Objectively there is much basis for an answer of no. Mass criminalization of minority and divergent cultures is deeply part of the national soul. Our institutions of justice have been successfully molded and corrupted in the reflection of our hate of illicit vice and untraditional culture. Our budget priorities, and so civic commitments, are a reflection of a public sector that has dwarfed the promise of community and progressive programs in the name of punitive abundance necessary to conduct the various domestic wars. The population has grown accustomed to prisons as a molding institution that rival and in some ways replace public schools.

Further we have come to accept that our criminal justice Constitutional promises are void. Indeed, for a generation we have purposefully selected Supreme Court justices who proudly promised to lend their interpretive weight in support of mass criminalization and the negation of police restraint. We have accepted that the Fourth Amendment's promise of personal privacy and restraint in police tactics is void by reason that it would inhibit triumph in the investigation of culturally forbidden nonviolent behaviors. We have undermined the promise of trial by jury because individual consideration is not compatible with mass criminalization. Similarly the other portions of the Constitutional ideal that would make the decision to punish a highly individualized determination stand abandoned. The defense bar has lost its place as a protected equal in a fair competition structured to render justice and instead is made a collateral enemy of the government. Jury convictions have become a rarity among the incarcerated. Grand juries have been perverted in fundamental mission, becoming tools of the prosecution rather than shields for the individual and community. The admonition of the Eighth Amendment, that punishment be kept from the dark human potential of cruelty, has fallen on a national mood to be proudly impervious to mercy. Politicians compete to show how little mercy, called weakness, is in their character. Similarly the warning against using standing armies to control and oppress are irrelevant. The nation has come to accept that it can only exist as an occupied police state. Double jeopardy has become a game rather than a right. The idea of an autonomous judiciary devoted to enduring promises rather than the passions of the day does not describe Constitutional law in relation to the War on Drugs. Equal protection in regard to the punishment state is similarly simply inapplicable.

Outside Constitutional law, the nation's solemn promises to other nations have been discarded with drug hate as the cause. Domestically the distinction between criminal law and civil law has been lost as forfeiture laws have become a second means to punishment when the criminal route is inconvenient or insufficient. Drug laws have come to dominate the docket, depriving the rest of society of a needed forum for dispute resolution.

This book has shown that though the War on Drugs is a public policy disaster, it has both supporters and beneficiaries. Some of whom continue to pump up the nation's hate at the old levels. If Ronald Reagan, William Bennett and George Bush all stoked hate and then retired, Barry McCaffrey, Joseph Califano and A. M. Rosenthal have tried to vie for their place as the new national hate team.

Yet as the replacement team at play in 1997 is compared in

competence and status to the gifted haters of 1980–1992, it must be said that the current wave is not up to their predecessors. Is a shift beginning, or shall a new more effective war party enter the field to renew the old campaign?

President Clinton by deed vies with the greats as a drug warrior. And yet here too there are signs of a changing of the guard. The drug for which he has shown genuine passion to reduce has not been counter-culture-linked marijuana, but the real killer, tobacco. Tobacco, rather than a drug of new age idealism, is linked to the old South and the old boys' money network of politics. He has deployed the Food and Drug Administration to assert regulatory authority and has worked to raise public awareness that tobacco is responsible for the deaths of twenty-fold more persons than all illegal drugs combined. As the public considers that the greatest drug merchants in the country use lawyers and accountants rather than guns and gangs, there is an inherent anti-drug war lesson to learn. On the traditional War on Drugs' substance of marijuana, Clinton has given mixed signals. On the youth-oriented medium of MTV he was even able to joke about his own "non-inhaling" experience. Laughter and hate rhetoric make a poor mix. Though he has asked Congress for $150 million for anti-marijuana propaganda, the issue is reactive with him, not where his instincts lead. All this said, the first four years of his administration coincided with the most arrests: 1 marijuana user was arrested every 54 seconds, and 1.5 million were arrested by the end of 1995.

The media has been shown to have participated and benefited from the hate phenomenon. As late as March 1996 another mass media drug event was launched. ABC declared the month its "March Against Drugs." The *Reader's Digest*, Partnership for a Drug Free America and Department of Education joined efforts for this mass gala. The culmination was "ABC-D Day," a program on March 31, 1996, that was meant to remind the viewer of the good old days of regular drug-bashing cop shows. ABC had their news and entertainment divisions construct anti-drug programming, while *Reader's Digest* published a promotion guide and Web site. The Department of Education underwrote the toll free telephone number and the Partnership provided advertisement.

A. M. Rosenthal, who devotes a syndicated column to bolstering the war effort, bemoaned in his review that the audience was so small as to set records for such broadcasting and to raise the question whether the drug war was over among the public. Further, many journalists expressed that it was time that drug policy coverage begin to acquire minimum notions of journalistic professionalism. Signatures to a letter demanding that ABC begin balancing its coverage of these issues included U.S. representatives Pete Stark (D-Calif.) and Maxine Waters (D-Calif.). In the heart of the drug war would leaders dared to have expressed a will for accuracy in the media?

More broadly, a more sober coverage of the issue has set in for much of the media. Reeves and Campbell report that Geraldo Rivera's two-hour syndicated special titled "American Vice: The Doping of the Nation" played a part in the reassessment. The more serious news and entertainment programs just could not compete in sensationalism with two hours of nonstop shooting action hyped by the host in a command center displaying maps of the nation as battlefield. And so they began to criticize the genre. Of at least as much significance, the Gulf War began. Networks had access to major league violence beautifully choreographed, filmed and presented without charge by the Pentagon. Local sheriffs with small guns and battering rams could not compete with cameras strapped to cruise missiles. And so the public shifted its entertainment diet to a more graphic presentation and never returned with the same gusto to the little domestic war. Again the War on Drugs' configuration showed signs of aging.

Both Bob Dole and George Bush rhetorically succeeded to out drug-hate Bill Clinton. Both found the strategy lacking in results. On the campaign trail Dole charged,

> the Clinton Administration surrendered, they raised the white flag on the War on Drugs. In the Dole Administration, we're going to return to what works. We're going to replace the President's inattention to dangerous drugs with a clear and forceful policy of zero tolerance. Zero tolerance for drug smugglers. Zero Tolerance for drug pushers. Zero tolerance for drugs in the workplace and drugs in school. And zero tolerance for drugs period. Zero! Zero!

> Zero! We will fully restore the office of the drug czar. We will redouble the efforts to put drug criminals behind bars. We will appoint judges who want to make tough, no-nonsense approach to drug offenders. We want tough judges who are sorry about the victims and not about the criminals. And every single person who works in my administration from the highest cabinet officer to the lowest official will speak with one voice—illegal drugs are completely and totally unacceptable and will be in a Dole-Kemp administration.[1]

Rhetorically Dole joined the drug-hate greats. Yet as for Bush before him, the old magic was missing. Had times changed in such a way that culture was ahead of politics which was ahead of policy which was still stuck in the midst of the war?

The question on some level seems absurd. Drug hate was the essence of politics for a generation. The coalition of beneficiaries and supporters of the war agenda seemed invincible. Drug hate seemed tied to the deepest American religious, racial, social and economic values. How then can the prospect of peace after such a popular war be considered?

Yet it does seem that the essential axis that holds each period of politics together in the twentieth century is, in turn, quickly rebuffed in the following period. Prohibition created a viable coalition that helped to unseat progressivism and bring in a reign of police rule. As the economy fell into depression, Roosevelt came forward, denounced Prohibition and freed resources and energy for a redistribution of the economy under the New Deal. McCarthyism then came along with its contrary call to hunt down people in positions of authority who felt fellowship with the poor and labor class. McCarthyism was in turn replaced by the Great Society as a will emerged to free the nation from the effects of racism, economic injustice and cultural sterility. The War on Drugs under Reagan was the rallying cry to again orient the public sector to its punishing capacity and abandon the aging Great Society ideas.

When each of the other central domestic policy agendas fell with the passing of the coalition that found it useful, why should the War on Drugs be the exception and continue on well past the demise of its founding era? Of Prohibition, McCarthyism and War on Drugs, the three punitive eras of twentieth-century politics, the first two were replaced with periods of renewed commitment to social justice. Is there a pattern that people do eventually dispel their anger and once again seek a government capable of good works or at least one disengaged from cultural warfare?

The most significant evidence in politics of a turning away from the angry righteousness expressed in drug policy is provided by the astounding results in two popular initiatives in the 1996 election. Both the people of Arizona and California voted to liberalize drug policy. Both did so over the objection of the state politicians, federal punitive bureaucracy and the Clinton administration, still stuck in drug war mentality.

The victory of these two initiatives is a fine contender for the title of the "David and Goliath" story of the political age. The full force of the old order, which built itself on the greater politics surrounding the hate, had every reason to believe it could belittle and dismiss these grassroots movements. Then on November 5, 1996, 2 out of 3 voters in Arizona supported the idea that drug use should be between a doctor and a patient rather than between a police officer and subject. In the nation's most populous state 56 percent of the public voted for the medical marijuana initiative.

The Arizona initiative is a broad and thoughtful repudiation of drug war anger and punitive excess. The initiative requires that persons serving prison terms at the time of the initiative for possession of controlled substances be released on parole unless the Board of Executive Clemency determined that the individual posed a danger to the general public. Released persons would be required to participate in a drug treatment or education program. Future persons convicted for possession of controlled substances would be eligible for probation rather than incarceration. They also would be required to participate in a drug education or treatment program. Medical doctors are allowed to prescribe controlled substances such as marijuana, heroin and LSD to treat diseases and relieve the pain of seriously ill persons. The doctor is required to be able to document that scientific research supports use of the controlled substances and must obtain a written second opinion also from a doctor concurring in the conclusion. The patient would then be exempt from criminal proceedings for possession and use of the controlled substance. Cost for running the treatment and education programs would be raised by a tax on alcohol, cigarettes and tobacco. That tax also raises funds for a public education campaign about drugs.

In sum the Arizona law, formally titled the *Drug Medicalization, Prevention and Control Act*, is a rational comprehensive reform of drug policy that substantially places drug use under a medical and educational model and significantly limits penal involvement in the policy area. The coalition that sponsored it was bi-partisan and not particularly counter-cultural in personality. The sponsoring committee, Arizonians for Drug Policy Reform, selected a Carter and a Reagan appointee as chair and treasurer. The central convictions of the group were that drug prohibition as practiced in the War on Drugs era was a comprehensive failure but that the alternative extreme of comprehensive legalization was both undesirable and politically unacceptable. They agreed as well that drug use was more a medical concern than a criminal problem. They expressed particular concern with the corruption of the police under prohibition, the overcrowding of prisons and the drain on public finance from mass incarceration.

A poll of the Arizona public revealed in 1996 that 91 percent believed the War on Drugs had been lost under the old strategies.[2] Fifty-five percent agreed that a shift in models from criminalization to education and treatment was called for. The Committee concluded that though the politicians of the state were unable to lead the public out of the era of failed policy, the public was ready to lead. In testimony before Congress to explain the decision of the people of Arizona, Marvin Cohen, former chairman of the Civil Aeronautics Board under President Carter, stated,

> Arizona voters have decided that it is time to return to rationality and deal with drugs in a way that can benefit rather than harm society. There is no reason to believe that the voters in the rest of the country support the failed

> drug war as it is currently being waged. We would hope that these hearings will initiate a re-examination that will bring federal drug laws and policies more in line with the will of the people of the United States.[3]

The referendum in California was less sweeping but even more shocking to the body politic precisely because California has led the trends in culture and politics in the second half of this century. The Compassionate Use Act provided that "seriously ill Californians have the right to obtain and use marijuana for medical purposes where the medical use is deemed appropriate and has been recommended by a physician who has determined that the person's health would benefit from the use of the marijuana in treatment of cancer, anorexia, AIDS, chronic pain, spasticity, glaucoma, arthritis, migraine or other illness for which marijuana provides relief." The patient, care giver, cultivator and physician are all freed from prosecution under state law.

Unlike Arizona, the California organizing group had roots in the hippie community that survived the drug war. The tolerant San Francisco police and district attorney had for years refused to implement criminalization against the city's successful and popular Cannabis Buyers Club. Under orders from the state's politically ambitious attorney general, Dan Lungren, state narcotic agents raided the establishment on August 4, 1996. Lungren from his days in Congress during the heart of the war had every reason to believe that active drug hate would be a successful political maneuver. This proved among the most spectacular political miscalculations in decades. One-third the voting public turned out to know personally someone who had employed marijuana to relieve suffering. Using strong-arm tactics on cancer and AIDS patients offended the moderate voter and expanded the coalition who supported the initiative. Gary Trudeau, author of the syndicated comic strip *Doonesbury*, publicized Lungren's bullying and received the best reaction he could have asked for. On October 1, 1996, Lungen held a news conference to angrily denounce the strip, raising the satire to prominent legitimacy. Trudeau subsequently spent another week driving home the absurdity of criminalizing the sick for seeking medicinal relief.

The state further exposed the weakness of its own arguments by falsely inserting the claim made by "No on 215" in the rebuttal argument that the American Cancer Society opposed the proposition. The Sacramento Superior Court ordered the lie removed. The American Cancer Society took no position on the initiative and had joined in petitioning to the Food and Drug Administration to allow the use of marijuana to relieve the suffering of cancer patients. Following that, Drug Czar Barry McCaffrey issued a public statement that "there is not a shred of scientific evidence that shows that smoked marijuana is useful or needed. This is not science. This is not medicine. This is a cruel hoax that sounds more like something out of a Cheech and Chong show." Several of the nation's most respected medical institutions formally attempted to publicly increase General McCaffrey's poor knowledge on the subject. With all this high profile exchange, the respected Field Poll discovered that six weeks before the election the majority of likely Californians had heard of the initiative and that they favored it by a 57 percent majority.

In the course of the campaign otherwise law-abiding citizens came forward to speak of their own benefits from the use of marijuana. Senior citizens from the most conservative sections of the state testifying that only smoked marijuana successfully relieved nausea after chemotherapy proved a powerful and persuasive argument. Their experiences reached the public through the efforts of a national network of drug policy reformers who for the first time in decades were beginning to show sophistication and resources.

The passage of these two initiatives created two reactions, both perhaps predictable. A number of science-based organizations responded positively that these initiatives finally opened the door to rational analyses after the long politicized hate era. Supporters of the drug war countered by personally attacking the proponents of the initiatives.

The prestigious *New England Journal of Medicine* advanced the cause of calm science in their 1997 editorial. They submitted that "thousands of patients with cancer, AIDS, and other diseases report they have obtained striking relief from these devastating symptoms by smoking marijuana. The alleviation of distress can be so striking that some patients and their families have been willing to risk a jail term." The editorial goes on to submit that "a federal policy that prohibits physicians from alleviating suffering by prescribing marijuana for seriously ill patients is misguided, heavy-handed, and inhumane."[4] They point out that unlike many drugs that doctors deal with, there is no concern of overdosing with this drug. That "federal officials are out of step with the public" and reflecting its proven use the drug should be reclassified. The similarly prestigious National Institutes of Health agreed that marijuana showed promise in treatment and the government should abandon its Schedule I ban on use and study.

The drug war bureaucracy took the opposite approach and tried to stamp out the initiatives and stomp on the backers. Janet Reno threatened on behalf of the United States that doctors who went ahead and recommended the use of marijuana could lose their right to issue prescriptions, be denied reimbursement for Medicare and Medicaid patients and face federal criminal charges.

The Drug Czar, William Bennett, stated that "These two propositions simply do not effect Federal law"; he went on the offensive, stating "there isn't a shred of evidence that smoked marijuana" is appropriate medicine and proclaimed, "That this initiative passed is a scandal. It's also understandable given the promotion and advertising that were used. Many of us would have been taken in."[5] Thus he dismissed the elective will of the people as irrelevant to his model of government.

Joseph Califano, President of the National Center on Addiction and Substance Abuse, vented rage against this break in the solid punitive model. One sponsor of these reform efforts was labeled by him as "the Daddy Warbucks of drug legalization"; he declared that the voters in the states "never had a chance. A moneyed out-of-state elite mounted a cynical and deceptive campaign."[6] To him the multibillion dollar per year drug war establishment was the outmatched underdog of the campaign.

The columnist A. M. Rosenthal was most vitriolic in the face of this breach in the war campaign. He warned that

> the determination to fight drugs actively is being drained and weakened and that we must start exacting a price from those who are doing it. . . . The Arizona and California victories for the marijuana "medicalization" propositions were bugles. The key players were the financier George Soros and his money. . . . The use of money does not have to be illegal to be contemptible or damage the country.[7]

George Soros, who did put up a quarter of the funds for these two small campaigns, responded, "I am not for legalizing hard drugs. I am for a saner drug policy. . . . I firmly believe that the war on drugs is doing more harm to our society than drug abuse itself."[8]

And so, amazingly, the drug warriors today after decades of propaganda feel the issue slipping from them. One poll taken after the passage of these initiatives found that 60 percent of American voters favor allowing doctors to prescribe marijuana.

Arizona state government has taken it upon itself to overrule the democratically spoken word of the people. The legislature passed a bill prohibiting doctors from recommending drugs not approved by the FDA. The Governor signed the bill into law and reduced clemency under the initiative from 1,000 inmates to 200 who must still appear before the Board of Executive Clemency. The People Have Spoken pro-initiative group has filed suit to have the initiative enforced.

Several California cities have alternatively acted to put Proposition 215 into effect. In San Francisco a new buyer's club opened with the approval of the city's district attorney and Department of Public Health. In April, 1997, federal agents of the DEA kicked down the doors, confiscated the plants and equipment and refused to press charges to avoid legal response. In San Jose the police department offered to try to negotiate with the federal authorities to leave their clinic alone.

The people of California spoke to this issue again in 1997 as a jury refused to criminalize a pot-smoking podiatrist for cultivating and smoking marijuana to relieve back pain. The case against Dr. Alan Ager was the first use of Medical Marijuana as a defense since the passage of the initiative. Two of the jurors refused to vote with the state and so protected the defendant with a mistrial. The scale of Dr. Ager's garden, 135 plants, might have labeled him as a dealer. Yet the jury spared him the wrath of the drug war.

The movement has spread, just as drug war enthusiasts feared it would. Six states have similar initiatives in process for the 1998 elections and several other states are considering the legalization of medical marijuana through legislative means.

Marijuana is the heart of the War on Drugs precisely because the criminalization of 600,000 Americans each year is nearly all about ideology and culture and emphatically not about health. Marijuana is the only drug specifically mentioned by Ronald Reagan in his drug war kickoff address. It is the drug that has remained the exception from any claim of government victory. There is no national drug crisis or reason for focus on drugs if marijuana is undemonized. All other drugs together have fewer than 2 million users, as opposed to 70 million people who have tried marijuana. Police budgets could no longer be justified and prison construction would end if marijuana ceased to be a crime. The acceptance of a legitimate medical use inevitably raises the question of how criminalizing of others for their use is conscionable. Medical sanction politically contradicts decades of propaganda that already stands contradicted by each person's personal experience. It certainly says that drug use and drug abuse are not synonymous. It also says that if the people lead against the war effort they actually can frustrate the great federal war machine. It creates the potential for dialogue rather than a "Just Say No" chant.

Chapters Four and Five attempted to explain how a policy to aggressively incarcerate many Americans for their illicit vice became so popular among even more Americans. This chapter turns to speculation on why this great engine of public policy may have finally run its course.

The explanation begins where Chapter Four left off. Drug use was popularized and romanticized as a portion of the general rebellion against the rules and norms of the pre-1960s explicitly racist, sexist, militarist, puritanic nation. Drugs became a symbolic and substantive act by which much of the population thought and declared itself free from the old constraints. Though the counter-culture achieved a great deal of attention, as well as some of its agenda, the larger population despised them for changing the old rules which were comfortable for many persons. As the dominant culture reasserted itself, initially under Nixon but much more vigorously under Reagan, the body politic did a very traditional thing and criminalized the opposition culture. Marijuana growers and users totaling in the millions were made to suffer the majority's backlash.

The point of this recital near the close of the millennium is to show what old news it all is. Both the hippies and their antagonists have aged and perhaps buried or at least reduced their commitment to opposition. A significant portion of the population has no personal involvement in the old conflicts over male hair length and female bra burning. For a significant share of the nation the Vietnam War and its peace activist antagonists are something out of the history books. The conflict between the cultural liberalism of the 1960s and conservatism of the 1980s is simply of less significance in the late 1990s and so one portion of the anger that fueled the domestic war has tempered.

Further, the reasons conservatives were able to argue that the nation was in decline as a result of the morals of the 1960s have also diminished. At the time of the launching of the conservative backlash, America feared itself to be losing its world standing. The Soviet Union had invaded Afghanistan, Iranian zealots held the American embassy hostage, and the oil embargo kept fuel prices high. Ronald Reagan promised to rid the country of the self-doubt and moral questioning the peace movement had raised. Revenge on this peace-mongering enemy within came for Reagan, as Nixon before him, through criminalization of its drugs of choice. Near the end of the Clinton administration America stands as the only super power, held in higher world stature than at any time in history.

Just so, toward the end of the Clinton administration the economy is at as fine an overall state as ever in history. Unemployment is low, as is inflation. The stock market exhibited an unprecedented 7-year growth surge as the benefits of new technology continuously pushed productivity. The percentage of Americans who own their own home hit an all time high. The federal government almost miraculously reduced its deficit spending to 15 percent of its high. Even violent crime, on the rise for decades, began an multi-year decline.

All this suggests a nation with much cause to become comfortable with itself. This undermines the political and social use of looking for internal deviance as the cause of moral and national decline. Dole, Bush and Lungren all had reason to learn that drug rage was no longer the political trump card of the prior era.

The War on Drugs was a battering ram to destroy the redistribution programs of the liberal era. By shifting the theory of social malady away from root causes such as limited education, limited opportunity and racism toward lack of personal responsibility as manifest in forbidden drug use, the drug war made way for the end of welfare, ridicule of the whole Great Society agenda and attack on affirmative action. The usefulness of the war in all these domestic agendas has come near an end. Welfare stands reformed nearly out of existence. Affirmative action is on decline through judicial and popular initiatives. The National Endowment for the Arts and the National Endowment for the Humanities have been humbled and reduced. An ideology of capitalism ungentled by government spending has become a broad consensus. There is simply less need in the conservative agenda for a battering ram to smash big government. Today that battering ram is what is big about government.

There is a growing belief in the Republican party that adoption of the intolerance agendas of the social conservative wing of the party is more a liability than an asset. Both Bush and Dole tried to free themselves from demands for criminalization of personal behavior in the platform writing process. Both discovered that the social conservative wings of their own party successfully punished them, forcing them to run on unpopular platforms and embarrassing them during the campaign. Both lost the general election in part because women in particular tend against voting for a President committed to the criminalization of abortion.

Governor William Weld of Massachusetts was nominated as ambassador to Mexico in 1997 and was blocked by Senator Jesse Helms because the Governor supports permitting the medical use of marijuana. A clash between Republicans who believe in deployment of mass police power to punish untraditional culture and believers in limited government and personal freedom is at hand.

Conservatism in most of the world means belief in a strong central government able to defend national orthodoxy with punitive authority. The War on Drugs is a genuinely conservative event on this world scale. Conservatism in America has had an alternative meaning of limited government, personal decision making, respect for the individual and laisse faire economics. The War on Drugs is comprehensively incompatible with this American tradition of conservatism. Conflict between these two antithetical notions of conservatism is a deep tension in the Republican party.

Democrats have alternatively attempted to join the war so that the surrounding righteous patriotism would not be deployed against them. They have witnessed the War on Drugs transform the big government they have built up since the time of Franklin Roosevelt from an array of agencies meant to provide support in the quality of life as an expression of modern liberalism to a punitively focused, traditionally defined conservative big government. To ransom their ideology of liberalism, defined as commitment of the public sector to enhancement of the quality of life, they must find the leadership to reject this surrender to unliberal values.

Despite the purposeful selection of a Supreme Court that is strikingly partisan to the domestic war, the Constitution by its inescapable nature, steeped in eighteenth-century liberalism, cannot be reconciled with armed police deployed for cultural control. Tension with the Constitution forms a whole front of problems for the war policy.

The fundamental clash between mass criminalization for cultural non-conformity and the Constitution remains the promise of a jury trial. The War on Drugs by necessity attempts to minimize this by circumventing the trial process and by instilling a high level of drug rage among the jury pool. Two factors have threatened this approach. One is the advent of minimum sentences that take away the ability of the state to buy back the Constitutional rights from the accused. The more important is the growing rebellion among some in the jury pool toward mass incarceration of minority youth.

In the simple numeric logic of voting and juries, majorities can structure the criminal code to criminalize the minority, but the minority can derail the infliction of punishment through the jury process. Traditionally only one dissenting vote from the jury prevented a verdict of guilty. The odds of a representative from the minority groups targeted under the drug war serving on the jury are high. These odds are multiplied when the statistical reluctance of busy educated middle-class people to serve on juries is added.

Part of the rebellion against criminalization among black jurors is a post–Rodney King graphic realization of the need to focus yet again on police behavior. Even before then judges began to notice and comment on the rising unwillingness for blacks to cooperate in the criminalization of other blacks. Reggie Walton, former assistant to William Bennett as Drug Czar, returned as a judge to the Washington, D.C. criminal court in 1991 and immediately noticed the change in black jury behavior. Cases in which the prosecution had clearly proven guilt against crack dealers routinely received a verdict of not guilty from the jury. He interviewed the jurors and was explicitly informed that there was a movement not to send any more young black men to prison for nonviolent offenses.[9]

Critical race theorists have long asked how it came to be that the criminal justice system had been transformed through drug policy into the acceptable means for implementing the worst of the nation's race sentiments. The answer they provide is that every level of the war effort has been tainted with racism. The laws were written to get blacks, the police, prosecutors and judges were selected to embrace the agenda and prisons were built in an age of diminishing public resources because racism is such a deeply held value. Professor Paul Butler of the George Washington University School of Law, a former federal prosecutor, has stated that the only response blacks can make is to recognize that they are usually the majority in urban juries, and that gives them the power to simply acquit all black males charged with nonviolent drug crimes.[10] Blacks, he submits, need to recognize that the laws, police, prosecutors and judges have all been targeted at them. The jury power is the legitimate means under the Constitution for the public to put the police authority on trial every time a conviction is sought by the government. As during the Rodney King and O. J. Simpson trials, the jury should consider their own experience with abuse in deciding whether to do the government's will and convict.

So common and shocking to the pro-incarceration judges is the rise of juries recognizing their powers that judges now routinely admonish juries that they have no right to bring moral convictions into the court room. The Federal Court of Appeals for the Second Circuit wrote in 1997 that "We categorically reject the idea that, in a society committed to the rule of law, jury nullification is desirable, or that courts may permit it to occur when it is in their power to prevent." In that instance a single black woman refused to allow the all-white jury to convict a black man on drug charges. The appeals court said a trial judge should dismiss a juror who insisted on bringing moral convictions into the court instead of relying strictly on evidence and the law as presented in court. Despite this will to undermine the jury deliberation, it is not difficult to appreciate that as sentiment turns against the war effort it is hard to monitor jurors. Traditionally jury deliberations are held in secret. Jurors can convict or acquit without interrogation of their reasoning.

Many judges have expressed realization that the laws as written give them no formal choice but to do injustice by immorally inflicting harm both to the defendant and the larger society. When judges are stripped by the written law of the authority to consider questions of justice they may well be appreciative of jurors finding the will to ask important questions.

The initiatives in California and Arizona as well as legislative acts from other states raise a field of Constitutional questions regarding federalism. Traditionally criminal law was a subject matter for the states. As the Reagan administration held the will to attack untraditional culture and to shift the federal role from Great Society helpfulness to conservative punitive government, the War on Drugs allowed Washington to take over the substantive field of criminal law. With the California initiative in particular, the federal government is actively seeking to use its powers to undermine the criminal law decision of the people of a state. The federal government has deployed federal agents to destroy a medicinal marijuana clinic that operated with the support of the San Francisco city government and it has threatened to use regulatory and criminal powers to punish doctors now operating under state law. The doctors have already filed legal action.

In 1997 the Supreme Court spoke in the matter of gun control ruling that the federal government cannot require local police authorities to implement the Brady bill by running a search on the history of gun buyers. Though support for gun proliferation is across the cultural divide from marijuana use, the question of forcing persons in the state to uphold the federal prohibition in abrogation of state law and city policy is surely coming.

Three times in recent years this current Supreme Court, selected for its hostile stance to limits on police authority, has found the behavior of drug war enthusiasts beyond even their boundaries. The first was already mentioned. The state of Wisconsin considered the Fourth Amendment rulings of the Court and determined that there existed an exception in deference to the drug war. Faced with this explicit language codifying the reasonable summation of the Supreme Court's own rulings, the justices balked.

Many states have attempted to reduce the cost of incarceration by turning the prison function over to private for-profit prison enterprises. These save money by paying the guards on a different scale and operating with fewer staff. The case of *Richardson v. McKnight* in 1997 threatens this whole cost-reduction effort.[11] The Supreme Court in an array of cases has shielded states from liability toward mistreated or harmed inmates. In *Richardson* they firmly refused to grant for-profit prison enterprises the immunity to harm prisoners or subject them to living conditions that threaten their basic health and then have the prison shielded from damages. Raising the cost of mass incarceration has long-term potential to undermine the popularity of punitive cultural crusades.

In *Chandler v. Miller* the Court finally broke ranks with the symbolism of the war.[12] The case reviewed a law in Georgia that candidates for state office must take a urine exam to be placed on the ballot. The Libertarian party candidate for Lieutenant Governor, who was both a party member and a lawyer, expressed his exasperation at having to give his urine to the state by calling the law an "asinine bunch of junk"; he explained, "alcoholism is obviously the worst drug problem among politicians . . . and there's no test for a politician's intelligence or ethics. Or the main addiction in political society—power."[13] Yet politicians look for advantage by posturing as tough in the endless and pointless drug campaign. In striking this law, the Court substantively rediscovered the Fourth Amendment in the drug context for the first time in decades. If the Fourth Amendment returns to the applied Constitution, the domestic war would be broadly prohibited.

An even greater challenge is posed by the emergence of an active judiciary. In the wake of denunciation of the Warren Court and liberalism of the 1960s and 1970s the judiciary was admonished to shift into a period of inactivity. Yet the 1996–1997 term was hardly one that could be characterized as inactive. The Court that year overturned a record number of federal laws, including the Brady Gun Control Act, Communications Decency Act and the Religious Tolerance Act. The War on Drugs fundamentally operates by stripping defendants and courts of their Constitutional prerogative to individual case determinations based on the due process of law. Even if this conservative Court is willing to abandon the rights of the accused, it may increasingly assert the fundamental prerogative of the judiciary. In the end though, if the judiciary insists on its own status as a separate co-equal branch entrusted to dispense justice on the case level, the individual gains the right to individual justice precluded by the wholesale criminalization required by the drug war. Mandatory sentencing, Three Strikes initiatives and the whole plea bargaining system take the courts out of their most vital role of providing individual determinations.

Such rebellion against diminution of the judicial role occurred in California in 1997 when the California Supreme Court ruled that despite the Three Strikes rule, judges have broad authority to reduce felony convictions to misdemeanors and so spare defendants harsh sentences. The court wrote that not to recognize such inherent power vested in the judiciary "would be one step shy of declaring the three strikes law eliminates the court's discretion entirely." This decision affirmed a ruling from a Los Angeles trial judge who reduced a drug conviction from a felony to a misdemeanor, allowing a Three Strikes defendant to receive probation rather than at least 25 years in prison.

At the most fundamental level, the Constitution promises an open society with a high level of guaranteed individual rights and limited police authority. The War on Drugs is a negation of these values. The more important the judiciary is, inherently the more it will find this conflict difficult to ignore. The nation will never get beyond the conflict between its most solemn promise and antithetical prohibition policies until it either formally suspends the Constitution or rejects the policies.

The Constitutional promises and structure of government thus join with popular rebellion and the passing of generational antagonism as forces that create the potential for the nation to reconsider its dysfunctional drug war convictions. Rational analyses and the pragmatic potential of the nation join these. The statistical and otherwise substantive argument that the War on Drugs has been a costly failure is overwhelming. This book began with recognition of three of the important substantive points: (1) the domestic war effort has corrupted the police, prison and judicial system, (2) government funds have been massively shifted from programs that help people to programs that hurt people and (3) mass criminalization has filled the nation with young minority men who are the product of the punitive system. If this is not enough, the litany of failure goes on.

For America's level of expenditure on criminal justice, this ought to be among the safest nations. Yet it is epically violent. The principal reason for this great failure of the criminal justice system is the dual mission imposed on criminal justice by the criminal codes. Added to the achievable mission of providing public safety and protecting property is the special mission of attempting to undo cultural change and deviance. The latter has proven an unwinnable directive that has soaked up the majority of criminal justice resources. Crimes against persons and property can be reduced through police deployment. Removing a thief or rapist from society reduces future incidences of those crimes. New rapists do not take up the crime because former rapists are incarcerated. Rather, prison has at least an incarceration effect and possibly a deferent effect as well. Crimes against culture have proven again and again extremely resistant to reduction through punitive force. The incarceration of a drug dealer, prostitute, gambling bookie or pornographer does not reduce the incidence of those behaviors. Rather, the markets for those products and services quickly adjust, leaving no reduction in undesired behavior and a host of damages and costs borne by society. The beginning of rationality in criminal justice is the recognition that society can have greatly increased safety of persons and property if it will only charge criminal justice exclusively with those tasks and leave issues of health and culture to doctors, educators and other more appropriate sources.

Drug use has proven particularly resistant to reduction by punitive means. America is the most punitive of the developed nations, yet it has the highest drug use and drug abuse rates. The nation's history, from Prohibition to the criminalization of prostitution, adultery, abortion and homosexuality, should have warned the architects of the drug prohibition that personal behavior has always proven highly resistant to control through punishment. After decades of punitive policy a long-term trend of return to broad drug use has set in.

The nation has deployed vast resources in a failed effort to reduce the world supply and importation of drugs. Though large quantities have been seized and many persons punished, these efforts have had a near-zero effect. Street prices of all drugs have dropped over the period of this intense effort, showing that importers actually suffer from too much of their goods getting through. In marijuana, the very pressure of large-scale eradication projects moved growing indoors, where significantly higher quality products are now raised. By dollar value, marijuana may be the nation's top crop. Mark Kleiman, a specialist on drug policy at the University of California at Los Angeles, submits "there's excess inventory and capacity at every stage."[14]

A third of the new AIDS patients have contracted the disease through needles. Rather than serving the interests of public health, the War on Drugs is a significant health problem. Methadone clinics have become a rarity over the drug war years, even as heroin achieved abundance in availability. While many doctors would like to prescribe marijuana, most are precluded or intimidated from doing so.

Hemp as a crop has failed in the United States because of the political fallout of the drug war. Hemp stalks could reshape the paper and apparel industries, reduce world deforestation and pesticide use, yield new building materials and provide nutrient-rich foods that reduce heart disease. International Paper Company, the world's largest paper producer, submits that hemp is the strongest natural fiber for paper. It is also the easiest to grow, has the broadest geographic range of any paper source and yields two to four times as much fiber per acre as wood. The nation had the wisdom to use hemp as a principal crop from colonial days till the 1930s when the crackdown on marijuana consumed the fiber use of the plant's stalk. Hemp returned to production during World War II as President Roosevelt launched the "Hemp for Victory" campaign to produce clothes and parachutes for soldiers. With the return of the drug prohibition after the war, the crop was again forbidden in the United States, though Europe and Asia have ignored America's objection and have expanded their production. Worldwide sales have moved from $5 million in 1993 to $75 million in 1995. One tracking firm estimates $600 million in sales by 2001.[15] Americans remain precluded from raising this valuable crop because of its drug obsession.

For a time during the cold war the United States was able to bully other nation's into at least mouthing support for the war effort. That tacit complicity has ended as the Soviet threat dimmed. Why drug hate is such a strong American passion and so unexportable to European allies is a fascinating inquiry. Part of the answer lies in the strength of American orthodox religions. Europe suffered for centuries under powerful churches. The age of Enlightenment was very much a rebellion against theocratic control. Today religion in France, England, Germany and many other countries provides important social and civic functions but is not allowed by popular will and in some instances by law to denounce human freedom in the name of God. Even in Italy and Ireland, where religion and nationalism are intertwined, the momentum is aggressively for secular liberation movements.

Americans like a moral absolutism which they get from the orthodox religious belief that their country is "one nation under God" with a mission in the divine scheme. This moral absolutism enforces the strong American tendency to create hard rules and declare wars on its own noncomplying behaviors. Europeans alternatively have come to accept that there is a broad diversity in human behavior and that it is wise to learn to live and let live. Imagine trying to explain to the French, America's series of dismissals in 1997 of high military officers for past adulterous affairs. Similarly, moral crusades against alcohol, prostitution, pornography or tobacco are examples of an American sociology of complete bafflement across the sea. Just so, there is no comparable demonization and politicalization of other drugs.

As racial and ethnic antagonism is a significant portion of why it is popular for Americans to declare war on each other, it is also a piece of why European nations with their comparative homogeneity decline to do so. In considering contemporary domestic policy, it seems Americans dislike each other and are willing to spend lavishly to hurt each other but are unwilling to spend to help each other. Europeans, alternatively, basically like each other and decline to spend on hurt but are willing to spend significantly to help.

European treatment of drugs shows that while the American drug war is irrational and destructive, there is no one public policy that is therefore right. All the European nations have come up with solutions that are more rational than America's continuing domestic crusade. The common refrain in the array of European policies is not to let drugs or other vice crimes dominate either criminal justice or larger public policy. There is a resolve not to let the response to vice compound the damage done to the nation. The Swiss, Dutch and British shrink the black-market and reduce the public health problems by making heroin and other drugs available by prescription to registered addicts. They allow doctors to treat patients with the full array of drugs without fear of the criminal justice system. Public information campaigns present honest information and so hold credibility among the population experienced with drugs. The publication on drug information sponsored by the British Department of Health writes in *Drug Abuse Briefing* that "the vast majority of people who use drugs come to no harm and may well feel that they benefited from the relaxation, diversion or temporarily improved social intellectual or physical performance that can be afforded by some drugs." Britain has half the drug use per capita of the United States. The Dutch allow for "smoking coffee shops" where marijuana is tolerated so long as the proprietors uphold public order. No European nation makes drugs into a serious public policy problem. There is no will to declare domestic war against their own populations.

All of these policies are generally described as Harms Reduction,[16] which is simply the claim that it is rational to admit that human behavior is not fundamentally transformed by law, and so public policy should be devoted to doing demonstrable public good and refraining from causing greater harm. The alternative American denunciation model celebrates punishment for punishment's sake, regardless of the lack of benefit and the observation of great harm. The benefit in the American model is intangible rather than empirical in the form of spiritual righteousness and defense of culture against change by punitive condemnation of deviance. Punishment in America has become a good in its own sake as a righteous denouncement of bad deviant culture rather than a tool measured by its effect on demonstrable social well-being. A Harms Reduction approach is simply the claim that punishment is a tool in public policy and should be so evaluated in deployment and continuation. Harms Reduction treats criminal policy as an extension of greater public policy rather than the separate fulfillment of patriotism or religious belief.

A Harms Reduction approach substitutes the prohibitionist question of what is the sinful nature of the forbidden behavior and what amount of punishment is due penance, for the question of, what is the real avoidable harm to society and how can rules be structured so that the non-conforming individual can be brought into the rules in a way to minimize social damage. An example is provided in American society by comparison of bar keepers to drug dealers. Both individuals sell drugs. Bar keeps do so under state licenses that require the proprietor to become an agent of the state, only selling to nonintoxicated persons over a designated age. These merchants compete by being friendly to customers, presenting clean and pleasant stores, and offering service and selection. Thus they are regulated and placed in a competitive environment that ought to minimize the harm their commerce does to society. The rules are fluid and can be changed at the public's will, such as the banning of advertising, or happy hours or the requirement of a bouncer to maintain public order. Disputes among parties in the transactions can be taken to the police, regulatory authorities or courts. Society can also impose the potential for private liability, thus deputizing the aggrieved parties to engage in legal action for the public's benefit. The enterprise is taxed to offset costs and to add funds to the general revenue.

Drug dealers, alternatively, are made the adversaries of the law and become a source of great social cost. Society loses all its ability to modify terms of the transactions and dealers will sell to anyone who has cash. Competition is defined by the violent staking-out of monopolistic turf. Disputes in transactions are routinely settled by violence. Society loses the ability to use liability to discourage harm. There is no taxation. Society has created a legal structure that fails to regulate the market and can only add to the inherent damage done by the drug use.

The power of the sheer reasonableness and logic of the claim that prohibition has only added to society's burden is the strongest force leading to abandonment of the failed and costly war effort. The public at large is aware of the simple truth that the war has amassed great costs with no benefit or end in sight. From there the question of how to deploy regulatory rules and agencies, educational campaigns, medical supervision, market forces, taxation and liability to achieve the least harm and greatest benefit is more complex and requires continuing adjustment. The nation has entered a period of creativity, reasoned analyses and compromise in tobacco use. The government and the companies are exploring terms for liability, taxation, regulation, advertising and disclosure. All this is done within the context of a realization that people like to smoke, grow and sell tobacco and will continue to do so for profit, pleasure, tradition, rebellion and out of addiction regardless of the disapproval of others. Prohibition is, hence, unreasonable, and society can only seek to modify the terms so to minimize harm. Can this reasonableness spread to relieve the nation of its drug war disasters?

In keeping with a Harms Reduction philosophy rather than a prohibitionist crusade, society seems ready to examine its commitment to the criminalization of clean needles. George Soros, who helped to finance the successful California and Arizona initiatives, donated $1 million in 1997 to hand out sterile needles to addicts. President Clinton's cabinet was split by the emergence of this issue. Health and Human Service Secretary, Donna Shalala, who has the power to lift the federal ban, said that needle exchange programs have been shown to slow the spread of AIDS. She is joined in her view by the American Medical Association, the American Bar Association and the U.S. Conference of Mayors.

Drug Czar McCaffrey was joined by the Family Research Council in denouncing the idea. Gary Bauer, President of this conservative religious lobby, called the proposal a "dopey idea, and Congress and the Clinton Administration would make a radical mistake to flirt with the idea of needle exchange programs as sound and effective policy."[17] Both the Harms Reduction advocates and the prohibitionists released contradictory polls in competing press conferences orchestrated to sway opinion in this drug war issue.

Looking for hope from within the pattern of nonparticipation in voting is an historic practice. The fact that usually only half the voters turn out for a major election and that the winner often only takes slightly over a quarter the total vote has inspired many analysts to consider the striking implications if only a small percentage overcome their alienation from the electoral system. The great tradition in this regard is to claim that someday the economic underclass will abandon their long term nonparticipation and America will have a worker's movement. Similarly, recognition of the statistical absence of Latino and black voters has raised the strategy of a Rainbow Coalition of nonwhites. It must be pointed out that despite the theoretical importance of these ideas, few elections have actually so won.

The fury of cultural antagonism played out in the War on Drugs, war on pornography, and attempts to criminalize abortion raise the question of whether there is the potential for a culturally based upturn in the electorate. The Post-Modernity project poll, introduced in Chapter 4, says that the demographic base most aggressively calling for mass criminalization of sin is already fully participatory in the electorate. The largest demographic group of all, designated the Permissivists, are alternatively the cluster least likely to participate. This group is nearly all baby-boomers or younger. Most are Generation Xers. Hence many have not hit the high participation years found in among the Traditionalists, who most despise the way culture has changed since their young adulthood in the 1950s and earlier. Permissivists believe in a more European life-style and a live-and-let-live philosophy but are alienated from politics. As Traditionalists, who perhaps will never become comfortable with the sexual revolution, feminism, multiculturalism, secular humanism and counter-culture, exit the electorate and are replaced with persons who participated in or were influenced by those social changes American politics might finally lose internal anger as its dominant characteristic.

A different demographic scenario for moving the country away from public policy that is based on dysfunctional internal anger draws on recognition that the culture wars at root are an expression of the majority feeling threatened by the emerging minorities. This raises the issue of what happens as there truly is no majority American demographic group. The War on Drugs is in part an expression of displacement by traditional whites as they saw their way of life end through modernity, multiculturalism and secularism. Yet though the policy rages on, is not the war lost? In the next decade blacks, Latinos and Asians will outnumber the total white population. The War on Drugs may have mustered more armed fire power than any of the other race-based oppressions in American history, but its demographic core is losing its majority. Perhaps the greatest public policy show of white dominance is also the last.

This book has focused on blacks as the principal victim group of the war, Latinos form an interesting aspect of hope for political realignment against the drug war on two intertwined fronts. America has settled into an annual practice of grading the nations of the Southern hemisphere on their level of adherence to the war effort. Sanctions may be brought to bear if too much tolerance is observed. This is a humiliating and unfriendly treatment of sovereign equals. The people of those nations have increasingly protested and the governments themselves have suggested that some of the drugs are part of traditional domestic culture and not an appropriate concern of the United States, the largest drug-producing and -exporting nation of all in the form of deadly tobacco. In Mexico and Colombia the drug dealers are often folk heroes, uniquely able to stand up to the northern bully. Latinos in the United States are a significant portion of the victims of the War on Drugs. The initial criminalization of marijuana was specifically targeted at them to break their numbers and strength in the Southwest. As displeasure with treatment of the home countries is added to domestic oppression, another source for the peace movement is added.

The values of liberalism came under thorough assault in the politics of the 1980s. Yet aside from politics, as American sociology is observed, a case can be made that liberalism is alive and well and that the life-style politics of the 1960s and 1970s weathered the storm, abandoned the political fray and continued on as a formidable and growing cultural wave. Marriage benefits for same-sex partners has become a norm in many employment settings. Discrimination against gays has become unacceptable in most locations. So too legal gender discrimination in education and employment has become rare. The battle over abortion, though still fought in some arenas, appears mostly to have been won by the liberals. A culture has been born in the last decade in defense of freedom of expression on the Internet. These are not issues of the downtrodden and sidelined. A powerful share of the public wants to make choices in their own lives. This demand is heard from both sides of the political spectrum, as libertarianism has joined with life-style leftism to question the use of government as punitive defenders of propriety.

Finally, when the War on Drugs is considered ultimately as the latest and one of the greatest battles in the unending human dialectic between those who cherish traditionalism and their natural antagonists who express devotion to boisterous creativity and disorderly newness, it is easy to realize that the war must end because the cycle achieves completion so that it may begin anew. The era of the drug culture rocked the rules and cherished order. Just as it seemed to the counter-culture that they had birthed the Age of Aquarius, opposing forces rose and forced a retreat from change in the name of a return to tradition and normalcy. The crusading forces for order have had a long, hard and successful campaign, but ultimately cannot conquer the human will for indulgence, rule breaking and creative non-conformity. Drugs, their abuses, uses, harms, quest inspiration and, most of all, conflicting symbolic value are a portion of the human composition that can never be successfully amputated. American society might learn to live with that as it forgives itself its diversity and human qualities.

NOTES

1. Rally Speech, Palos Park, IL, Aug. 25, 1966.
2. *Drug Policy News Letter*, Number 32, Spring 1997.
3. Testimony before U.S. Senate Judiciary Committee, Dec. 2, 1996.
4. *New England Journal of Medicine*, Jan. 30, 1997.
5. *Drug Policy Letter*, Number 32, Winter/Spring 1997.
6. Ibid.
7. Ibid.
8. Ibid.
9. Dan Baum, *Smoke and Mirrors*, Boston, Little Brown, 325.
10. "Black Scholars View Society With Prism of Race," *New York Times*, May 5, 1997.
11. Docket # 96–5955 (1997).

12. 65 L.W. 4243 (1997).

13. "Libertarian Takes Fight Against Drug-Test to Supreme Court," *New York Times*, April 7, 1997.

14. "Why Seizing Drugs Barely Dents Supply," *New York Times*, Dec. 15, 1996.

15. "Getting a Financial High From Rope," *Washington Post Weekly Edition*, Jan. 13, 1997.

16. See Franklin Zimring, *The Search for Rational Drug Control* (New York, Cambridge University Press, 1992).

17. "White House Warned Not to Fund Free Needles," *San Francisco Chronicle*, Aug. 21, 1997.

Selected Bibliography

Bartee, Wayne. *Litigating Morality: American Legal Thought and Its English Roots*. New York: Praeger, 1992.

Baum, Dan. *Smoke and Mirrors: The War on Drugs and the Politics of Failure*. Boston: Little Brown, 1996.

Braithaite, John. *Not Just Desserts: A Republican Theory of Criminal Justice*. New York: Oxford University Press, 1990.

Caute, David. *The Year of the Barricades*. New York: Harper and Row, 1988.

Decker, John. *Revolution to the Right: Criminal Procedure Jurisprudence During the Burger-Rehnquist Court Era*. New York: Garland, 1992.

Dumm, Thomas. *Democracy and Punishment*. Madison: University of Wisconsin Press, 1987.

Gitlin, Todd. *The Sixties: Years of Hope, Days of Rage*. New York: Bantam Books, 1987.

Gusfield, Joseph. *Symbolic Crusade: Status, Politics and the American Temperance Movement*. Urbana: University of Illinois Press, 1963.

Hagan, John. *Deterrence Reconsidered*. Beverly Hills: Sage Publications, 1982.

Inciardi, James. *The War on Drugs*. Mountain View, CA: Mayfield, 1992.

Johnson, Haynes. *Sleepwalking Through History: America in the Reagan Years*. New York: W. W. Norton, 1991.

Klienman, Mark A. R. *Marijuana, Costs of Abuse, Costs of Control*. Westport, CT: Greenwood, 1989.

Krauss, Melvin B. and Edward P. Lazear. *Searching for Alternatives: Drug Control Policy in the United States*. Palo Alto, CA: Hoover Institution Press, 1991.

Mathiesen, Thomas. *Prison on Trial: A Critical Assessment*. London, Newbury Park: Sage Publications, 1990.

Meier, Kenneth. *The Politics of Sin*. Armonk, NY: M. E. Sharp, 1994.

Messner, Steven and Richard Rosenfeld. *Crime and the American Dream*. Belmont, CA: Wadsworth, 1994.

Miller, James. *The Passion of Michel Foucault*. New York: Simon and Schuster, 1993.

O'Brien, David M. *Privacy, Law and Public Policy*. New York: Praeger, 1979.

Orman, John. *The Politics of Rock Music*. Chicago: Nelson Hall, 1984.

Perry, Charles. *The Haight-Ashbury: A History*. New York: Vintage, 1985.

Primorac, Igor. *Justifying Legal Punishment*. Atlantic Highlands, NJ: Humanities Press International, 1989.

Reeves, Jimmie and Richard Campbell. *Cracked Coverage: Television News, The Anti-Cocaine Crusade, and the Reagan Legacy*. Durham: Duke University Press, 1994.

Richards, David A. *Sex, Drugs, Death and the Law*. Totowa, NJ: Rowman and Littlefield, 1982.

Rorabaugh, W. J. *Berkeley at War: The 1960s*. Oxford: Oxford University Press, 1989.

Sadofsky, David. *The Question of Privacy in Public Policy: An Analysis of the Reagan-Bush Era*. Westport, CT: Praeger, 1993.

Schlesinger, Arthur, Jr. *The Cycles of American History*. Boston: Houghton Mifflin, 1986.

Schwartz, Bernard. *The New Right and the Constitution*. Boston: Northeastern University Press, 1990.

Shaw, David. *The Pleasure Police*. New York: Doubleday, 1996.

Siegel, Ronald. *Intoxication*. New York: E. P. Dutton, 1989.

Stevens, Jay. *Storming Heaven: LSD and the American Dream*. New York: Atlantic Monthly Press, 1987.

Stinchombe, Arthur. *Crime and Punishment: Changing Attitudes in America*. San Francisco: Jossey-Bass, 1980.

Wilson, James Q. and Richard J. Hernstein. *Crime and Human Nature*. New York: Touchstone, 1985.

Zimring, Franklin. *Prison Population and Criminal Justice Policy in California*. Berkeley: University of California Press, 1992.

Index

About the Author

DAVID SADOFSKY BAGGINS is Associate Professor of Political Science at California State University at Hayward. Among his earlier publications are *The Question of Privacy in Public Policy: An Analysis of the Reagan-Bush Era* (Praeger, 1993) and *Knowledge as Power* (Praeger, 1990).

ISBN 0-275-95956-2

90000>

EAN

9 780275 959562

HARDCOVER BAR CODE